Brushing Up English to Learn Greek

Brushing Up English to Learn Greek

By
PETER S. PERRY

RESOURCE *Publications* • Eugene, Oregon

BRUSHING UP ENGLISH TO LEARN GREEK

Copyright © 2014 Peter S. Perry. All rights reserved. Except for brief quotations in critical publications or reviews, no part of this book may be reproduced in any manner without prior written permission from the publisher. Write: Permissions. Wipf and Stock Publishers, 199 W. 8th Ave., Suite 3, Eugene, OR 97401.

Resource Publications
An Imprint of Wipf and Stock Publishers
199 W. 8th Ave., Suite 3
Eugene, OR 97401

www.wipfandstock.com

ISBN 13: 978-1-4982-0635-8

Manufactured in the U.S.A.   11/18/2014

All translations are the author's unless otherwise noted.

New Revised Standard Version Bible (NRSV), copyright 1989, Division of Christian Education of the National Council of the Churches of Christ in the United States of America. Used by permission. All rights reserved.

Gloria Dei

with gratitude to Greek students at
the Lutheran School of Theology at Chicago, 2007–2013

Contents

Introduction | ix

1. **Grammar Jargon** | 1
2. **Verbs—the Action Words** | 8
3. **Continuous Active Indicative Present** | 19
4. **Nominative and Accusative Cases** | 23
5. **Genitive and Dative Cases** | 31
6. **Adjectives** | 38
7. **Prepositions—Fine Tuning Relationships** | 42
8. **Pronouns—Standing in for Nouns** | 48
9. **Passive Voice** | 52
10. **Middle Voice** | 56
11. **Continuous Past** | 64
12. **Future Time** | 68
13. **Aorist Aspect** | 72
14. **Perfect Aspect** | 78
15. **Participles** | 84
16. **Subjunctive—the Mood of Possibility** | 89
17. **Infinitives—the Verbal Noun** | 95
18. **Imperatives** | 100
19. **Relative Pronouns—Relating a Clause to a Noun** | 105

Appendix: For Further Study of Greek Aspect | 111

Answer Key to Exercises | 113

Glossary | 139

Bibliography | 145

Introduction

English Grammar can be the biggest obstacle to learning Greek. We use so much jargon to talk about a language, words like "noun," "verb," "morphology," and "syntax" that sound foreign in themselves. Many of us may remember these from grade school but the memories may have become foggy from time and disuse. This book is written for foggy memories that need a brush up before learning Greek.

Each chapter begins with a devotion to center us on the grace of God, without which we could not do anything. Each topic receives a brief introduction before discussing the similarities and differences between English and Greek. Finally, there are exercises to practice the grammar skills discussed in each chapter.

My suggestion is to completely but quickly read the chapter and get to working exercises at the end of each chapter. As you work exercises, it may be helpful to refer back to the chapter material. After giving it a good try, check your answer with the answer key in the back. Make sure you understand the answer—talk to a classmate or the instructor if you have questions. This material is fundamental to making sense of Greek, so do what it takes for you to understand it well.

Credit goes to Samuel Lamerson (*English Grammar to Ace New Testament Greek*) for the basic structure of each chapter. I relied on Joseph M. Williams (*Style: Ten Lessons in Clarity and Grace*) for insights into English grammar. For English-Greek comparisons, I drew on H. P. V. Nunn (*A Short Syntax of New Testament Greek*) and Harvey Bluedorn (*A Review of English Grammar for Students of Biblical Greek*).

The following table will help coordinate this book with popular grammars, N. Clayton Croy's *A Primer of Biblical Greek* and William Mounce's *Basics of Biblical Greek* (3rd ed, abbreviated *BBG*).

Brushing Up	Croy *Primer* Chapter	Mounce *BBG* Chapter
1. Grammar Jargon	1	5
2. Verbs	2	15
3. Continuous Active Indicative Present	2	16
4. Nominative and Accusative	3–4	6
5. Genitive and Dative	5	7
6. Adjectives	6	9
7. Prepositions	6	8

INTRODUCTION

8. Pronouns	7	11–12
9. Passive Voice	9	18
10. Middle Voice	9	18
11. Continuous Past	10–11	21
12. Future Time	12	19
13. Aorist Aspect	13–14	22–23
14. Perfect Aspect	15	25
15. Participles	18	26
16. Subjunctive Mood	23	31
17. Infinitives	24	32
18. Imperatives	18	33
19. Relative Pronouns	27	14

1

Grammar Jargon

DEVOTION

For I received from the Lord what I also handed on to you, that the Lord Jesus on the night when he was betrayed took a loaf of bread... (1 Cor 11:23)

Ἐγὼ γὰρ παρέλαβον ἀπὸ τοῦ κυρίου, ὃ καὶ παρέδωκα ὑμῖν, ὅτι ὁ κύριος Ἰησοῦς ἐν τῇ νυκτὶ ᾗ παρεδίδετο ἔλαβεν ἄρτον...

These are the first few words of what we call "the Words of Institution," as Paul taught them to a Christian community in the Greek city of Corinth. Some Christians were treating the communal meal as their own private dinner. As a result, some were going hungry while others became drunk (11:21–22). Paul's solution was to remind them of the words Jesus used to institute the meal. They had heard the words before but needed to hear them again. The words point their attention at Jesus and the community gathered as his body. Before they eat, they should "discern the body" (11:29), that is, become aware of whole community as Jesus' body and the bread and wine as his body and blood. They cannot gather and eat the Lord's Supper as some kind of private meal because there is one body and blood that Jesus gave for the whole community. Paul uses the words they have received to persuade them how to behave when they gather.

In Christian communities, the words of the New Testament have been received and handed on for generations. They didn't digest all those words at once, but were shaped by them over repeated hearing and use. By the grace of God, the words of the New Testament are handed on to us so that God can work in us and through us. As we begin our study of the Greek New Testament, we will study these words in new ways, praying that the Holy Spirit make us one body gathered around the Word and the Sacraments.

INTRODUCTION: PARTS OF SPEECH

Although jargon can be an obstacle, we need special words to talk about how a language works and to make comparisons with other languages. Taking time now to understand the jargon will help maximize understanding. I will mark words found in the glossary at the back of the book with an asterisk (*).

*Grammar is the study of the basic principles of a language, which include *Morphology and *Syntax, and the meaning commonly inferred from forming and arranging words.

*Morphology is the way individual words are formed *(morphē* = "form" in Greek).

Jesus walked on the seashore.

"Walked" is the correct *morphology of the word "walk" to describe an action in the past. What is an example of another form of this word?

*Syntax is the way that multiple words are arranged to form sentences (*syn* = together; *taxis* = arrangement). The following sentence is an example of incorrect English *syntax. What is the correct syntax?

Jesus walked the seashore from.

*Parts of Speech are some ways to classify words based on their common function. We will discuss nine: *Noun, *Pronoun, *Adjective, *Verb, *Adverb, *Preposition, *Conjunction, *Interjection, *Article. If we think of a sentence as a dramatic play, words are the actors in the play. They have customary parts to play, which we call "parts of speech."[1]

A ***Noun** is a name for anything. Another way to detect a noun is to see if it can fill in this blank: "*The _____ is good.*" Some nouns are concrete, such as boat, rock, and net. Others are abstract: love, joy, and peace. Some nouns are derived from adjectives or verbs: "Decision" is derived from the verb "decide." "Happiness" is derived from the adjective "happy." This sentence has two nouns: Jesus and seashore:

Jesus walked on the seashore.

A ***Pronoun** is a word that stands in for a noun. The noun that is replaced is called the ***antecedent**. Some pronouns include "I," "you," "they," "who," "that," and "this."

Jesus walked on the seashore. He saw Peter and Andrew fishing.

"He" stands in for Jesus; therefore, the sentence could be rewritten, "Jesus saw Peter and Andrew fishing."

An ***Adjective** is a word used with a noun to describe it, indicate it, or count the number. Another way to detect an adjective is to put the word *very* in front of it (there are some

---

1. This metaphor helps us to separate the customary roles of words from their actual function in a specific sentence. Context rules!

exceptions!). Adjectives often answer the questions: *What kind? How many? How much? Which? Whose? In what order?*

Jesus walked on the <u>sandy</u> seashore.

The net was <u>full</u>.

A ***Verb** is a word used to make a statement about a *noun, ask a question, or make a command. It must agree with the *subject in *person and *number. A *Verb Phrase includes helping words (sometimes called auxiliaries or modals) such as "shall," "can," "may," "might," "should," "would," "must," and "ought to." Some verbs (such as "is," "have," "do," and "get") may function as auxiliaries. For our purposes now, be able to identify the whole verb phrase and don't worry about auxiliaries.

Jesus <u>walked</u> on the seashore.

Andrew <u>asked</u>, "Where <u>are</u> you <u>going</u>?"

Mary <u>said</u>, "<u>Come</u>! Our Lord <u>has been raised</u>."

An ***Adverb** is a word that modifies all parts of speech except *nouns. Adverbs often answer *When? Where? How?* or intensify a word. In English, many adverbs end in "-ly."

The storm was <u>extremely</u> large.

The adverb "extremely" intensifies the adjective "large"

Jesus <u>frequently</u> taught in the synagogue.

"Frequently" modifies the verb "taught" answering the question *when?*

The disciples moved <u>very</u> <u>slowly</u>.

"Very" intensifies the adverb "slowly."

A ***Preposition** is a word that indicates the relationship between two *nouns (or equivalents). It is followed by a word or phrase we call **the object of the preposition**. Together this phrase is called a ***prepositional phrase**, and functions as either an *adjective or *adverb. Another test of a preposition is that it can be placed before "her" and "them" but not "she" and "they."

Jesus walked <u>on</u> the seashore.

"On the seashore" is the prepositional phrase. "On" describes the relationship between "Jesus" and "seashore," answering the question *where* Jesus walked.

In the beginning was the Word.

"In" is the preposition. "The beginning" is the object of the preposition. So, you would identify "in the beginning" as the prepositional phrase. What is the prepositional phrase in the following sentence?

They said, "He eats with tax collectors and sinners."

A ***Conjunction** is a word that joins *sentences, *clauses, *phrases, or words. When you see a conjunction ask what it connects. "And," "but," and "or" are the three most common, but "because," "although," "thus," "therefore," "as," and "while" are also conjunctions in English. The main idea is that they link words, phrases, and clauses.

In this example, "and" connects two words:

Peter and Andrew followed Jesus.

Here, "or" connects two phrases ("through Judea" and "through Idumea"):

He did not travel through Judea or through Idumea.

In this case, "but" connects two clauses (each clause has a subject and verb):

Others saw him but they did not follow.

Consider the conjunction "as," which in this example connects the first half of the sentence to the second half.

As he went a little farther, he saw James and John.

An ***Interjection** is a word thrown into a sentence to express a feeling. It has no grammatical relationship with any other word.

Behold! I will tell you a mystery!

Amen! Come, Lord Jesus!

***Articles** are joined to nouns like adjectives. They are easier to list than define: the definite article is "the," and in English we use "a" or "an" as indefinite articles. (There is no indefinite article in Greek.)

Grammar Jargon

A man came from God.

This person is unknown to the audience, so he is introduced with the indefinite article.

The net was full of fish.

The speaker is referring to a particular net, known or assumed to be known by the audience.

OTHER TERMS TO KNOW

The *****Person** of a verb or pronoun indicates the relationship with the speaker or audience. There are three classes of persons:

1st person   "I" or "we" (the speaker refers to her- or himself)
2nd person   "you" (the speaker refers to the audience, singular or plural)
3rd person   "she," "he," "it" (singular) or "they" (plural) (the speaker refers to someone or something other than self or audience)

The *****Number** of a noun, pronoun, or verb indicates whether it is **singular** or **plural**.

The *****Subject** is what the *verb agrees with in number, or, another way to say it, the subject is what determines whether the verb is singular or plural. One way to find the verb is to put **what** or **who** in front of the verb and turn it into a question. The answer to the question is the subject. The **whole subject** may be more than one word. It is critical for comprehension to be able to detect the whole subject.

The assembly gathered together.
Who gathered?

He was brought to their council.
Who was brought?

Flesh and blood cannot inherit the kingdom of God.
What cannot inherit?

The *****Predicate** is everything that follows the *subject, beginning with the *verb.

The assembly gathered together.

He was brought to their council.

Flesh and blood cannot inherit the kingdom of God.

The ***Lexical** form of a word is the way you will find a word if you look it up in a lexicon (such as BDAG, the abbreviation of the lexicon edited by Bauer, Danker, Arndt, Gingrich) or in the back of most introductory grammars, such as Croy's *Primer* (p. 244 for the "Greek to English Vocabulary") or Mounce's *BBG* (p. 394 for the "Lexicon").

EXERCISES

Exercises in each chapter are ordered from easiest to hardest. Check your answers using the answer key at the end of the book. If you have questions, jot them down to include in a discussion.

Identify the part of speech of each word in the following sentences.
1. Jesus went beside the sea.

2. The whole crowd gathered around him and he taught them.

3. As he was walking along, he saw Levi.

4. The wedding guests do not fast while the bridegroom is with them, do they?

5. The Pharisees said to him, "Look! Why are they doing what is not lawful on the Sabbath?"

Identify the subject and predicate of the following sentences. Be sure to indicate the whole subject—it may be more than one word.
6. Jesus departed with his disciples to the sea.

7. John the baptizer appeared in the wilderness.

8. A great multitude from Galilee followed him.

9. People from the whole Judean countryside and all the people of Jerusalem were going out to him.

10. That evening, at sundown, they brought to him all who were sick or possessed with demons.

2

Verbs—the Action Words

DEVOTION

and he sustains all things by the verb of his power . . . (Heb 1:3)

φέρων τε τὰ πάντα τῷ ῥήματι τῆς δυνάμεως αὐτοῦ . . .

The NRSV translates this verse, "and he sustains all things by his powerful *word* . . ." τό ῥῆμα is often translated as "word," but is also the Greek word for the verb, the part of speech that indicates the subject's action. By using τό ῥῆμα, the author of Hebrews emphasizes that the Son's words are action words. When the Son speaks, it is an active word. Something happens! Here, the universe ("all things") are sustained by means of the verb of his power. It is Christ's action word that bears God's power to sustain, forgive, and renew the universe, all things, even us.

DEFINITIONS

A ***Finite verb** is a word used to make a statement about a *noun, ask a question, or make a command. It is called "finite" because it refers to a specific noun (the subject) and must agree with that *subject in *person and *number. Later we will learn about verbal forms that are not finite (such as *infinitives and *participles), meaning they do not have *person or *number.

A ***verb phrase** includes helping words (sometimes called auxiliaries or modals) such as "shall," "can," "may," "might," "should," "would," "must," and "ought to." Some verbs (such as "is," "have," "do," and "get") may function as auxiliaries. For our purposes now, be able to identify the whole verb phrase.

Verbs—The Action Words

AN OVERVIEW OF SIMILARITIES AND DIFFERENCES

1. Both Greek and English use verbs to make statements, ask questions, and give commands. Consider the following, using the verb "walk":

Jesus walked near the sea. (A statement about Jesus, the subject)

Did Jesus walk near the sea? (A question about Jesus, the subject)

Walk near the sea, Jesus! (A command to Jesus)

2. In English and Greek, the form of the verb changes (is ***inflected**) depending on its aspect, voice, mood, time, person, and number. In English the inflection may be evident in the verb but more often by adding auxiliary verbs (such as "did," "does," "have," "had," etc.). In Greek, the verb is inflected much more, and English translations will often have to add auxiliaries.

Take our three examples above: To make "walk" past time in English we inflect the word by adding "-ed":

Jesus <u>walked</u> near the sea.

To ask a question in past time, we began the question with "did." The *verb phrase is "did walk." In English questions, the subject is usually the second word in the sentence:

<u>Did</u> Jesus <u>walk</u> near the sea?

To make a command, the subject of the verb is "you," but this is usually omitted in English and Greek. The identity of "you" may be clarified by adding the person's name (in the nominative or the vocative case in Greek):

(You) <u>walk</u> near the sea, Jesus!

3. You may have learned that English verbs have *tense. For many Greek textbooks, "tense" is the word used. The problem is that when we think of "tense" in English we too quickly think about time. H. P. V. Nunn writes,

> It is somewhat unfortunate that we are compelled to use the name tense in connection with the forms of the Greek verb. It directs our attention too much to the **time** of the action of the verb, whereas it was the **state** of the action, rather than the time, that was most prominently before the mind of a Greek.[1]

---

1. Nunn, *Short Syntax*, 66, his emphasis. See Croy, *Primer*, 7–8; Mounce, *BBG*, 124.

What Nunn calls "state" and others call "kind of action," we will call "aspect." For learning Greek we will say that tense refers to two intertwined concepts: *aspect and *time. The important thing to remember is that:

Tense = Aspect + Time

Every verb in Greek has *aspect (including non-finite forms), but only verbs in the *indicative mood have *time (see below). You will need to remember this as you read your Greek grammar textbook. For indicative verbs, when he says "tense," think "aspect + time." For non-indicative moods (like the subjunctive), when you see "tense" in Greek textbooks write "aspect." Because *aspect is so exegetically significant in Greek, we will follow a trend in scholarship that distinguishes aspect and tense.

Aspect

4. *****Aspect** refers to the verb's point of view of the action, especially in respect to continuity and completion.[2] Every verbal form (finite and non-finite) has aspect in Greek.

4a. The *****Continuous Aspect** (some people call it "progressive" or "incomplete") describes a point of view inside the action, with no sense of its completion, beginning, or end. In English the continuous aspect is expressed using an auxiliary verb (usually some form of "be," such as "am," "are," "was," etc.) and a participle (a verbal form with -ing). For example,

Jesus is walking near the sea.

Notice how there is no sense of Jesus' completion of walking, the beginning of the walk, or the end of the walk. Jesus is in process of walking.

This aspect can be represented by a straight line:

―――――――――

The continuous aspect also can suggest habitual or repeated action without sense of beginning or end. In this case, English does not express the continuous aspect except by the implication of habit or repetition:

Jesus teaches every Sabbath.

---

2. For further discussion of Greek aspect, see the Appendix and Bibliography.

Verbs—the Action Words

In this case, the continuous aspect can be represented by a series of dashes:

4b. The ***Aorist Aspect** indicates "simple" or "undefined" action. In Greek, the word "aorist" means "undefined." This aspect is undefined in the sense that its viewpoint must be determined in context. However, we can say generally that the aorist aspect views the action from the outside, and may focus on various parts of the action or the action as a whole. It may view the beginning of the action, its end, or the whole action. In English, we have a similar "simple" aspect:

Jesus walked near the sea.

It is not clear without context if "walked" refers to the beginning, end, or the whole event. Like Greek, this is undefined without more context. Unlike Greek, the above English sentence could be continuous if the context suggested that Jesus did this habitually. Greek would make the aspect clear by the form of the verb.

Many Greek textbooks will talk about the aorist as if it always refers to past time. It is true that a logical way to view a whole event, its beginning, or end is when it has happened in the past. So, many forms of the Aorist aspect we will see in past time. No aorist forms in Greek will be marked in present time (although in English the simple aspect is used in present time). We will see Aorist Passive Future forms.

A key point to remember is that only indicative forms have time. Other moods are not marked for time, for example, the imperative and subjunctive moods, as well as infinitives and participles. In these forms, the aorist aspect is very significant.

We will discuss this further when we get to the aorist (chapter 13). For now, it is important to visualize the aorist in contrast to the continuous and perfect aspects. The aorist is undefined and can refer to:

(1) the **beginning** of an action (represented by an arrow at the beginning of the line):

_____
↑

(2) the **end** of an action (represented by an arrow at the end of a line):

_____
                ↑

(3) or the **whole** action (represented solely by a dot):

•
↑

4c. The ***Perfect Aspect** (or "completed") emphasizes an action that has reached its natural conclusion and has some enduring effect or result. In English, we add forms of the auxiliary "have" to a participle to make the perfect aspect:

Jesus has walked near the sea.

The English does not carry the same force as the Greek, however. In Greek, the perfect aspect may emphasize some effect of Jesus walking, depending on the context.

For example, in Greek the verb "write" often is used in the perfect aspect because the act of writing produces something enduring when the action reaches its natural conclusion:

Matthew has written a gospel.

In Greek, the verbal form translated as "has written" emphasizes that the action has reached its natural conclusion (i.e., the gospel was finished) and has enduring effects (i.e., the written gospel is here in front of us). This sense is difficult to translate into English, but is exegetically significant.

We will discuss this further when we get to the perfect aspect. For now, the key is to think of the perfect like a dot (the completed action) followed by a line of enduring effects up until a certain point:

•_____
↑

Voice

5. ***Voice** refers to the relationship between the grammatical *subject of the verb and the *agent of the action.

5a. The *****Active Voice** communicates that the *subject is the same as the *agent. The *agent is the one who does the action. For example:

Matthew wrote a gospel.

"Matthew" is the subject of the verb "wrote" **and** the agent who did the action of writing.

5b. The ***Passive Voice**, on the other hand, communicates that the ***subject of the verb is the direct object of the action**. In English, we use some form of "be" with a past participle. In Greek the passive voice is indicated in the form of the verb. In English and Greek, the agent may be omitted or communicated using the preposition "by" (ὑπό in Greek). For example:

A gospel was written.

The grammatical subject is "gospel." Who did the writing? The agent is omitted.

A gospel was written by Matthew.

Here the agent is communicated using the prepositional phrase "by Matthew."

We will find the use of the passive voice often to be exegetically significant because it generally emphasizes the object of the verb over the agent of the action.

5c. The ***Middle Voice** does not have an equivalent in English. Its use in Greek was fading about the time the New Testament was written and so there are few true middle verbs in the NT.

Although there are few true middle voice verbs in the NT, there are a number of important verbs that are middle voice in form and *active voice in meaning. These are called ***Deponent** verbs (**middle in form, active in meaning**). *Deponent is not technically a voice, but I encourage you to note "deponent" when parsing these verbs. We will cover the middle voice in chapter 10.

Mood

6. The ***Mood** of a verb expresses the speaker/author's perception of the reality of the action of the verb. The indicative, imperative, subjunctive, and optative are all finite forms (they have person and number). Although infinitives and participles aren't technically moods, it is traditional to include these non-finite forms under the category of mood.

6a. The ***Indicative** mood is used for ordinary statements and questions. It "indicates" something, expressing or inquiring about reality or facts. The indicative mood is generally the only mood with *time (discussed further below). For example:

Jesus <u>walks</u> near the sea.

<u>Did</u> Jesus <u>walk</u> near the sea?

6b. The ***Imperative** mood is used for commands and instructions towards establishing a fact or reality. For example:

Walk near the sea!

Write the gospel.

6c. The ***Subjunctive** mood expresses potential rather than actual facts. In general, we use auxiliaries like "may" or "might" with the verb for the subjunctive in English. This is somewhat an unreliable way to translate the Greek subjunctive, but don't worry about that now. The subjunctive is especially important in some conditional statements ("if . . .then"). We will cover all this more in later chapters.

Jesus may walk near the sea.

If Matthew were to write a gospel, then I will read it.

6d. The ***Optative** mood is rare in the NT. It is used to express a wish or hope for reality. The most common in the NT is μὴ γένοιτο, usually translated "By no means!"

Should we continue in sin in order that grace may abound? By no means! (Romans 6:1)

6e. *ced**Infinitives** are verbal nouns. In English, we add "to" before a verb to make an infinitive. Infinitives are non-finite, meaning they do not have a person or number. For example:

To err is human.

"To err" is an infinitive, functioning as the subject of the verb "is."

6f. *****Participles** are verbal adjectives. In English, we generally add "-ing" to the verb to make a participle. For example,

I saw the man walking near the sea.

"walking" is a participle, here modifying "man." Like an adjective it answers the question "which man."

Time

7. *****Time** applies only to verbs in the *indicative mood that indicate facts or ask questions.

7a. *****Past** time refers to an action that happened prior to the time when the speaker spoke the sentence.

Verbs—the Action Words

Jesus <u>walked</u> near the sea.

From the point of view of the speaker of this sentence, Jesus walked in the past.

7b. *__Present__ time refers to action contemporary with speaking.

Jesus <u>walks</u> near the sea.

As the speaker speaks these words, Jesus walks. In storytelling, the present tense is sometimes used to help the audience feel as if the story is taking place at that very minute, even if it refers to past events. This is called the *__Historic Present__. In the New Testament this is common with verbs of speaking:

And Jesus <u>says</u> to the disciples, "Believe in me!"

7c. *__Future__ time refers to action that, at the time of speaking, has not yet taken place. In English, we generally add "will" to the verb to indicate future time.

Jesus <u>will walk</u> near the sea.

Person and Number

Finite verb forms (i.e., not infinitives or participles) express *Person and *Number. The subject should match the verb's person and number. If there not an explicit subject, the subject is indicated by the verb form. To review:

The *Number of the finite verb is either singular or plural. The *Person of a pronoun indicates the relationship with the speaker or audience. There are three classes of persons:

1st person	"I" or "we" (the speaker refers to her- or himself, singular or plural)
2nd person	"you" (the speaker refers to the audience, singular or plural)
3rd person	"she," "he," "it" (singular) or "they" (plural) (the speaker refers to someone or something other than self or audience)

The "Greek Verb Parsing Chart" that follows this section should be memorized so that you easily remember the options to consider as you parse verbs.

The *Lexical form of a verb is the way you will find it if you look it up in a lexicon or in the back of your Greek grammar textbook. *Turn to the lexicon at the back of your Greek textbook (e.g., Croy p. 244 or Mounce p. 395) and note how verbs appear.* *Verbs are shown with their principal parts, always in the Indicative First Person Singular. The first entry is the Continuous Present; the second, the Continuous Future; the third, the Aorist Past; the fourth, the Perfect Active Present; fifth, Perfect Middle/Passive Present; sixth,

Aorist Passive Past. The point is that the lexicon entry will quickly let you see how the stem changes according to aspect, voice and time. For example:

ἀγαπά-ω, ἀγαπήσω, ἠγάπησα, ἠγάπηκα, ἠγάπημαι, ἠγαπήθην, I love

When writing your vocabulary cards, add a dash between the stem and the ending. It will help you see the difference between the stem and ending, remember that it is the lexical form, and that it is uninflected. (For example, ἀγαπάω is not a real Greek word, it is only the lexical form!) Also, it will help you to recognize *deponent verbs that will have -ομαι endings in the lexicon (we will discuss this more in chapter 10).

For example, write on one side of your vocabulary card:

ἀγαπά-ω

and "I love" on the other side. When you are making vocabulary cards from your Greek textbook, you will need to add the dash to each verb.

Verbs — the Action Words

Greek Verb Parsing Chart

Aspect	Voice	Mood	Time (only for Indicative)	Person (not with infinitive or participle)	Number (not with inf. or part.)	Case (Participles)	Number (Ptcpls)	Gender (Ptcpls)
Continuous	Active	Indicative	Present	1st	Singular			
Aorist	Middle	Subjunctive	Past	2nd	Plural			
Perfect	Passive	Optative	Future	3rd				
	*Deponent	Imperative						
		Infinitive						
		Participle				Nom	Singular	Masc
						Gen	Plural	Fem
						Dat		Neuter
						Acc		

We are dividing **tense** into two parts, **aspect and time**. When you read "tense" in Greek textbooks, grammars, and commentaries, think "aspect and time."

For example, when you read:
"Present Tense" think Continuous Aspect + Present Time.
"Imperfect Tense" think Continuous Aspect + Past Time.
"Pluperfect Tense" think Perfect Aspect + Past Time.

Every verbal form has Aspect, Voice and Mood.
 Indicative moods will include time, person and number.
 Subjunctives, optatives, and imperatives will include person and number.
 Infinitives will only have aspect, voice, and mood.
 Participles have verbal features (aspect, voice, and mood) and adjectival features (case, number, and gender).

Aspect: the speaker's point of view on the action of the verb.
 Continuous: Internal to the action, no view of beginning or end. Action in progress.
 Aorist: Literally, "undefined" without context. External to the action, may view beginning, end, or whole action.
 Perfect: Action has reached natural completion and has continuing effects at the time indicated.

*__Deponent__ is middle/passive in form, active in meaning. (It is technically not a voice, but helpful to note when parsing.) See chapter 10 for more information.

EXERCISES

Circle the finite verb(s) in English, that is, verbs that have person and number. Be sure you circle the whole *verb phrase, which may be more than one word. If the finite verb is an auxiliary (am, are, be, do, have, had, etc.) with another verbal form (e.g., a participle ending in "-ing"), circle that too. These words may be separated in English, but often will be communicated by one word in Greek! Next to each finite verb write its time (past, present, future), person (1st, 2nd, 3rd) and number (singular, plural).

1. When he entered the temple, the chief priests came to him.

2. They said, "By what authority are you doing these things?"

3. Jesus said to them, "I will also ask you one question."

4. If you tell me the answer, then I will also tell you.

5. Did the baptism of John come from heaven?

6. And they argued with one another.

7. They said, "If we say, 'From heaven,' he will say to us, . . ."

8. "Why did you not believe him?"

9. We are afraid of the crowd, because they all regard John as a prophet.

10. So they answered Jesus, "We do not know."

3

Continuous Active Indicative Present

DEVOTION

For the one whom God has sent *is speaking* the verbs of God . . . (John 3:34)

ὃν γὰρ ἀπέστειλεν ὁ θεος τὰ ῥήματα τοῦ θεοῦ λαλεῖ . . .

John's gospel emphasizes that Jesus is "the one whom God has sent." Two disciples ask where he comes from (1:38) and he says, "Come and see!" He also might have said, "Come and hear!" because John portrays Jesus as speaking so much (consider his dialogues with Nicodemus, the Woman at the Well, the Jews about the Bread from heaven and then Abraham, and the "Farewell Discourse").

The continuous aspect of λαλεῖ (here translated "is speaking") emphasizes that Jesus is in process of speaking. Jesus' words are not complete at this point in the story, by any means. The stress is on the continuous nature of Jesus speaking. He is continually speaking the verbs of God, the action words through which God is bringing light and life to the world. Through John's gospel and our proclamation of it, Jesus continues to speak the verbs of God, the message of life to us and the world.

DEFINITION: THE CONTINUOUS ASPECT

The *continuous aspect (or progressive or incomplete) describes a point of view inside the action of the verb, with no sense of its completion, beginning, or end. In English the continuous aspect is expressed using an auxiliary verb (usually some form of "be," such as "am," "are," "was," etc.) and a participle (a verbal form with "-ing").

This aspect can be represented by a straight line:

———————

If referring to a habitual or repeated action, the continuous aspect can be represented by a series of dashes:

The *active voice communicates that the *subject is the same as the *agent. The *agent is the one who does the action.

The *indicative mood is used for ordinary statements and questions. It "indicates" something, referring to actual facts in time. The indicative mood is generally the only mood with *time.

*Present time indicates that the verb's action is contemporary with the speaker/author's utterance.

SIMILARITIES

1. Both Greek and English have a continuous or progressive aspect that emphasizes that the action is on-going without any reference to completion, beginning, or end. In English we typically add some form of "be" to a present participle (ending in "-ing"):

Jesus is talking to the disciples.

This sentence does not give any information about the completion of Jesus' talk, when he began or when he might end. It expresses the on-going nature of the action. Jesus is in process of talking.

With more context, this might have a durative sense, such as that Jesus has been talking for awhile or keeps repeating himself. **Context rules!**

2. Your default translation of the Continuous Active Indicative Present into English should include some form of "be" with a participle ending in "-ing":

Ἰησοῦς λέγει· ἐγώ εἰμι τὸ φῶς τοῦ κόσμου.

Jesus is saying, "I am the light of the world."

DIFFERENCES

1. Present time in Greek can be used to express vividly an event in the past or future. This gives a "happening right now" feeling that storytellers love to create. We call this the *historic present. For example,

Continuous Active Indicative Present

καὶ <u>ἔρχονται</u> πάλιν εἰς Ἱεροσόλυμα.

A rough translation would be

And they <u>are coming</u> again into Jerusalem.

This translation correctly expresses the storyteller's effect. This kind of rough translation is where you should start, and after you gain confidence you can translate it into smoother English. With the *historic present we often would use the past in English: "And they came again into Jerusalem."

2. The continuous aspect in Greek also can have a simple meaning in some contexts.

Ἰησοῦς <u>ἀκούει</u> τοῦ δούλου.

If the context implies that Jesus is in process of listening to the slave speaking, then we would translate this sentence as:

Jesus <u>is hearing</u> the slave.

If the context suggests the action is simple, or not continuous, it may be translated:

Jesus <u>hears</u> the slave.

As said above, your default translation of the Greek continuous aspect into English should stress the continuous aspect. Then you can ask if that emphasis makes sense in context. Remember that **context rules**!

EXERCISES

Rewrite the following sentences in English to emphasize continuous action of the verb. In general, you will need to use some form of "be" with a participle.

1. Jesus returns to Capernaum.

2. Many people gather around the home.

3. He speaks the word to them.

4. Four people bring a paralyzed man to him.

5. They dig through the roof above him.

6. They let down the mat.

7. Jesus forgives the man's sins.

8. Some scribes question in their hearts.

9. Jesus perceives their thoughts.

10. The man stands up and takes the mat.

4

Nominative and Accusative Cases

DEVOTION

For "Everyone who calls on the name of the Lord shall be saved." (Romans 10:13)

πᾶς γὰρ ὅς ἂν ἐπικαλέσηται τὸ ὄνομα κυρίου σωθήσεται.

τὸ ὄνομα is appropriately translated as "the name" into English, but when talking about Greek grammar τὸ ὄνομα is also the word for "the noun." A noun is nothing but a name for something, a word that describes but also limits the possibilities for understanding something. If you printed this page out, we might refer to it as a "paper." The word "paper" gives it a name, and focuses our attention on its relationship with other things we call "paper" while minimizing other relationships. By calling it a "paper" we focus on its material. If we called it "assignment" we would focus on its relationship to you as a student in this class. In other words, nouns are names that describe and prioritize relationships.

Paul quotes the Greek translation of Joel 3:5 to provide evidence that "Everyone who calls on the name of the Lord shall be saved." The name of the Lord (or perhaps the "noun of the Lord") describes God as the one who saves through Jesus Christ, who may be called upon so that "there may be righteousness for everyone who believes" (10:4). To call upon the name of the Lord is to be in relationship with God through Christ, focusing our attention on God as the source of salvation and righteousness and minimizing any other relationship that may claim that place in our lives.

On our journey to learn Greek, this quote reminds us of the importance of our relationship with God through Christ. Our righteousness does not come from learning Greek (thank God!).

Yet, the quote also reminds us of the importance of translating the words of scripture into a language that can be understood and believed so that others will be in relationship with God. Paul used the Greek translation of Joel, which was originally in Hebrew, to make this point. We will learn how to translate Greek into English so that we also may proclaim "Jesus is Lord" and many may believe.

BRUSHING UP ENGLISH TO LEARN GREEK

INTRODUCTION: ENGLISH CASES

A *Case is a form of a word that signals its function in the sentence. In English, *pronouns are the best example. Note the underlined words:

He went to the sea.

Jesus put mud on his eyes.

Peter called out to him.

"He," "his," and "him" are three forms of the 3rd person, singular, masculine pronoun in English. Each signals a function:

He is the subject of the verb in the sentence "He went to the sea."

His indicates who possesses the eyes in the phrase "on his eyes."

Him indicates the recipient of Peter's calling.

When a word changes form based on its function, it is said to be *inflected, from a Latin root which means "bent." A summary of the way the form of a word changes when customarily used is called a *declension. For example, here is the declension of pronouns in English:

	1st Sing.	2nd Sing.	3rd Masc, Sing.	3rd Fem, Sing	1st Plural	2nd Plural	3rd Plural
Subjective	I	You	he	she	we	you	they
Possessive	My	your	his	her	our	your	their
Objective	Me	you	him	her	us	you	them

Note that sometimes a form is used in many different ways. For example, the word "you" can be either subject or object, singular, or plural! It is impossible to decide the case of "you" without the context of a sentence. With the following sentences, we can decide the case:

You were following Jesus. ("You" is the subjective case)

I gave the message to you. ("You" is the objective case)

Without even more context we can't tell who "you" refers to, and whether or not it is singular or plural. This leads to an important rule for both English and Greek:

Nominative and Accusative Cases

Context rules!

Although we will learn how words are customarily used, the specific function of a word can only be determined in context.

PARSING

*Parsing is describing the form of a word. For each part of speech there is a scheme for parsing, like blanks to be filled. For *articles, *nouns, and *adjectives there are four blanks to fill in:

Case: _____   Number: _____   Gender: _____   Lexical Form: _____

The *Lexical Form is the form of the word that you will find in a dictionary.

The <u>women</u> led the way to the river.
women = *case:* subjective; *number:* plural; *gender:* feminine; *lex. form:* woman

Jesus picked up the <u>rock</u>.
rock = *case:* objective; *number:* singular; *gender:* neuter; *lex. form:* rock.

We have included "gender" as a category for parsing, although it means something different in English than it does in Greek. In English, the rock is an "it" because it is not male or female. This is "natural gender." In Greek, "gender" does not necessarily match the "natural gender" of a word.

DEFINITION: THE NOMINATIVE CASE

In Greek the *Nominative Case is most commonly used to indicate the subject of a verb. One way to remember this:

The nominative case nominates the subject.

The nominative case is also the *lexical form for *nouns and *adjectives.

SIMILARITIES

Functionally, the English subjective case is equivalent to the Greek nominative case. Both indicate the subject of the sentence.

DIFFERENCES

In general, English *articles, *nouns, and *adjectives do not have different forms for each gender. Greek uses three genders: **Masculine, Feminine, and Neuter.** This is different from English, which uses "natural gender" (as discussed above). In Greek, when we say that λόγος ("speech" or "word") is Nominative, Masculine, Singular, the "gender" is grammatical and does not imply that the word is male.

In Greek, it is easier to determine the case of a word than in English! Since the word changes form based on case, there is very little duplication of forms. However, this means that there are more forms to memorize.

Word order is another difference. In English, the subject almost always comes before the verb. In Greek, the subject (in the nominative case) can appear anywhere in the sentence.

TRANSLATION PROCEDURE

First, read a Greek sentence out loud up to a punctuation mark or a word that introduces a new clause (the most common are ὅτι or ἵνα). This will help you avoid the mistake of trying to translate it one word after another. **Greek word order is primarily for emphasis not syntax!** Restrain your impulse to translate one word after another. Read aloud to consider the whole clause and look for the subject and verb anywhere in the clause.

Next, look for the subject. Sometimes there is no word in the nominative case, which means that the subject is indicated by the ending of the verb. If you can't find a separate subject, move on to step three and find the indicative verb.

<u>Translation Steps</u>
STEP 1: Read the Greek clause out loud up to punctuation, ὅτι or ἵνα
STEP 2: Look for the subject (in the nominative case) & translate subject.
STEP 3: Find indicative verb, parse and translate verb.
STEP 4: Translate the rest of the clause.

Check your work by matching the number and person of the subject to the ending of the noun. They should match!

RECOGNIZING THE NOMINATIVE

The easiest way to recognize the nominative case is to first look for an article.

Articles are your best friends!

When you are looking for the subject, look for an article in the nominative case. The subject will follow close after it! Notice the rough breathing mark in four of six forms.

Nominative and Accusative Cases

Nominative Definite Articles

	Singular			Plural		
	Masc	Fem	Neut	Masc	Fem	Neut
	ὁ	ἡ	τό	οἱ	αἱ	τά
Pronounce:	haw	hey	taw	hoi	hai	ta

Memorize these first! Know them in your sleep! They are all primarily translated as "the" into English, but recognizing them quickly will make learning Greek easier.

Examples:

<u>ὁ λόγος</u> ἦν πρὸς τὸν θεόν.
<u>The word</u> was with God. (John 1:1)
<u>ὁ λόγος</u> = nominative, singular, masculine; lexical form = <u>λόγος</u>

<u>ἡ ζωὴ</u> ἦν τὸ φῶς τῶν ἀνθρώπων.
<u>The life</u> was the light of the people. (John 1:4)
<u>ἡ ζωὴ</u> = nominative, singular, feminine; lexical form = <u>ζωὴ</u>

<u>τὸ φῶς</u> ἐν τῇ σκοτίᾳ φαίνει.
<u>The light</u> in the darkness shines. (John 1:5)
<u>τὸ φῶς</u> = nominative, singular, neuter; lexical form = <u>φῶς</u>

Eventually you will need to memorize the case endings, but start by knowing and recognizing the articles.

INTRODUCTION: DIRECT OBJECTS

The Direct Object of a sentence in English usually occurs after the *verb and answers *what* or *whom* receives the action of the verb.

Moses hit <u>the rock.</u>

The direct object is "the rock" because it answers what was hit.

Jesus saw <u>Peter and Andrew.</u>

The direct object is "Peter and Andrew" because it answers the question *who* was seen.

DEFINITION: THE ACCUSATIVE CASE

In Greek, the *__Accusative Case__ most commonly signals the direct object. Most broadly, however, the *accusative limits the action of a verb in terms of extent, direction or goal. With prepositions, for example, the *accusative often signals **motion towards**.

SIMILARITIES

In general, when you see a word in the *accusative the first guess should be that it is the direct object of the verb.

Keep in mind, however, the broader definition of the accusative so you won't be surprised. Even in English, the direct object carries the sense of limiting the verb by extent, direction, or goal. For example, in the sentence "Moses hit the rock," "the rock" limits the extent of the hitting action and also specifies the direction of the hitting.

DIFFERENCES

Unlike English, the Greek *accusative is used beyond the direct object. You do not need to memorize these other uses right now, but only be aware that the accusative limits the verb in terms of extent, direction, or goal. For example:

1. With prepositions, the accusative often signals **motion towards**.

Allow the children to come towards me.
ἄφετε τὰ παιδία ἔρχεσθαι πρός με.

2. The accusative is used to indicate the **subject of an infinitive**.

Allow the children to come towards me.
ἄφετε τὰ παιδία ἔρχεσθαι πρός με.

3. With units of time, the accusative indicates the **duration** (extent of time).

... fasting forty days and forty nights ...
... νηστεύσας ἡμέρας τεσσεράκοντα καὶ νύκτας τεσσεράκοντα ...

4. The accusative can function as an **adverb**, modifying the verb.

Finally, my brothers, rejoice in the Lord.
τὸ λοιπόν, ἀδελφοί μου, χαίρετε ἐν κυρίῳ.

Nominative and Accusative Cases

RECOGNITION OF THE ACCUSATIVE

Knowing the accusative definite articles will aid recognition of accusative nouns:

<u>Accusative Definite Articles</u>

	Singular			Plural		
	Masc	Fem	Neut	Masc	Fem	Neut
	τόν	τήν	τό	τούς	τάς	τά
Pronounce:	tawn	teyn	taw	tous	tas	ta

The *Lexical form of a noun is the way you will find it if you look it up in a lexicon or in the back of your Greek textbook. *Turn to the lexicon in the back of your textbook (e.g., Croy p. 244 or Mounce p. 395) and note how nouns appear.*

*Nouns normally have only one gender. Their *lexical form is the nominative case with the appropriate definite article following. For example:

ἀγάπη, ἡ, love

ἀγάπη is a feminine noun, as indicated by the nominative feminine definite article ἡ. When you are making your vocabulary cards, be sure to write the noun with the article.

EXERCISES

Look at the underlined English word and use the names of Greek cases (only nominative or accusative for these examples) to *parse the underlined word, giving the case, number, gender, and *lexical form (in English). The idea is to begin to think in Greek categories. For these examples we'll follow English gender, so list the gender as neuter unless it is "naturally" masculine or feminine. Write "?" when it is not possible to determine the number or gender without more context.

1. <u>John</u> was standing with two of his disciples.

   Case: _____ Number: _____ Gender: _____ Lexical Form: _____

2. The two disciples heard <u>him</u>.

   Case: _____ Number: _____ Gender: _____ Lexical Form: _____

3. The <u>speech</u> of Christ stirred my heart.

   Case: _____   Number: _____   Gender: _____   Lexical Form: _____

4. A Samaritan <u>woman</u> came to draw water.

   Case: _____   Number: _____   Gender: _____   Lexical Form: _____

5. <u>The disciples</u> were urging Jesus to eat something.

   Case: _____   Number: _____   Gender: _____   Lexical Form: _____

6. For by grace <u>you</u> have been saved through faith.
   Τῇ γὰρ χάριτί ἐστε σεσῳσμένοι διὰ πίστεως· (Eph 2:8)

   Case: _____   Number: _____   Gender: _____   Lexical Form: _____

7. And they sent to him their <u>disciples</u> . . .
   καὶ ἀποστέλλουσιν αὐτῷ τοὺς <u>μαθητὰς</u> αὐτῶν . . . (Matt 22:16)

   Case: _____   Number: _____   Gender: _____   Lexical Form: _____

8. And getting <u>a sponge</u>, filling it with sour wine . . .
   λαβὼν <u>σπόγγον</u> πλήσας τε ὄξους . . . (Matt 27:48)

   Case: _____   Number: _____   Gender: _____   Lexical Form: _____

9. <u>They</u> went into the house of Simon and Andrew.
   ἦλθον εἰς τὴν οἰκίαν Σίμωνος καὶ Ἀνδρέου. (Mark 1:29)

   Case: _____   Number: _____   Gender: _____   Lexical Form: _____

10. Are <u>you</u> greater than our father Jacob?
    μὴ σὺ μείζων εἶ τοῦ πατρὸς ἡμῶν Ἰακώβ; (John 4:2)

    Case: _____   Number: _____   Gender: _____   Lexical Form: _____

5

Genitive and Dative Cases

DEVOTION

"And it happened as the angels went away from them into heaven, the shepherds were speaking to one another, "Let us travel indeed until Bethlehem and let us see this word/event that has happened, which the Lord made known to us." (Luke 2:15)

Καὶ ἐγένετο ὡς ἀπῆλθον ἀπ᾿αὐτῶν εἰς τὸν οὐρανὸν οἱ ἄγγελοι, οἱ ποιμένες ἐλάλουν πρὸς ἀλλήλους· διέλθωμεν δὴ ἕως Βηθλέεμ καὶ ἴδωμεν τὸ ῥῆμα τοῦτο τὸ γεγονὸς ὃ ὁ κύριος ἐγνώρισεν ἡμῖν.

It's a well known story: the angels appear to the shepherds and dazzle them with heavenly pyrotechnics and biblical (literally!) proclamations of divine benefaction. They rush off to see what the angels were talking about.

Except the whole verse is not necessary to the plot of this story. Verse 15 could have been cleanly omitted, thus moving directly from the angelic pronouncement to the description in verse 16: "And they went, making haste, and discovered Mary and Joseph and the infant . . ." We as readers and hearers would have assumed that the angels went away and the shepherds decided to check it out. What does verse 15 do?

First, it highlights the shepherds as believing and eager respondents to the divine word. Recall that Zechariah didn't believe Gabriel that he'd have a son (1:20). Mary's first question was "How can this be . . . ?" (1:34). These shepherds have no hesitation, but even before the angels have disappeared, they are already making plans to go to Bethlehem. They believe and they act on what they have heard.

Second, the dialogue between the shepherds focuses our attention on the source of the revelation: the Lord (see Acts 2:28 for a similar construction). The final clause ("which the Lord made known to us") makes clear that the shepherds have experienced a "word" (see 1:37, 38, 65) from the Lord. This word is "to us." The pronoun is a first-person dative plural, here functioning as an indirect object. The Lord is the subject; the event they witnessed is the direct object. They are the recipients.

We too are "indirect objects" receiving the revelation of God through the Bible. When we first face learning Greek, we may feel like a bunch of shepherds facing an angel of the divine, but the message to us is that God's gracious will is to us and for us. We don't know where this new adventure will lead us. Like the shepherds who go to Bethlehem with only a few sentences but hearts full of faith, we go to learn and read the Bible that we may "see this word that the Lord has made known to us."

INTRODUCTION: ENGLISH "OF"

In English, we can use the word "of" in many ways:

This book of mine was once Francine's.

Here, "of" signals **possession**, even as the apostrophe-s ('s) at the end of Francine does. "This book of mine" could be rewritten, "my book," using the possessive form (inflection) of the pronoun.

I am buying a glass of soda.

The "of" here signals **content**: the glass is full of soda.

One who lives in a house of glass shouldn't throw stones.

The house is not filled with glass in this case. Instead, the **material** of the house is glass.

Who shall separate us from the love of Christ?

"Love" is a noun that is derived from a verb, what some call a "verbal noun." Sometimes the sense of verbal nouns followed by "of" can be found by substituting the "of" phrase with a subordinate clause. For example, try "Christ" as subject of the verb love in a clause beginning with "that": "Who shall separate us from the love *that Christ loves*?" And as object: "Who shall separate us from the love *that loves Christ*." Clearly the first makes sense: Christ is doing the loving, and so he is the "subject" of the verbal noun "love." This is an example of the **subjective** use.

The speech of Christ is life to the world.

This example demonstrates an ambiguous use of "of." "Speech" is probably not a thing that can be possessed. It could be **subjective** and rewritten with "Christ" as the subject of an action: "The speech *that Christ speaks* is life to the world." This could make sense, depending on the context. Remember that context rules.

It also could be **objective**, meaning "Christ" is the object of the verbal action: "The speech *that speaks Christ* is life to the world." This suggests that Christ is the object of the speech. Often when the "of" is objective, it can be replaced by "about": "The speech *about* Christ is life to the world."

"Of" could also point to the **source** of the speech. In this case, the "of" can be replaced by "from": "The speech *from* Christ is life to the world." In this example, this is very close to the subjective sense.

To decide between these three options, more context is required to clarify what is meant.

One of us will come to visit you soon.

This is different than other examples listed above. Here, "of" signals that one person is part of a larger group. We call this the **partitive** use because it separates one part from a group.

DEFINITION: THE GENITIVE CASE

"Of" is the keyword to remember for the Greek Genitive case. It will be helpful to remember the broad range of the meaning of "of" in English as you consider how to translate the genitive in Greek.

Generally, the genitive case is adjectival or descriptive, which means that a noun in the genitive case is usually connected with another noun and qualifies that noun. Memorize the two basic functions:

1. Kind (default translation "of...")

For you all are children of light.
πάντες γὰρ ὑμεῖς υἱοὶ φωτός ἐστε.

2. Separation (default translation "from...")

Shake the dust from your feet.
ἐκτινάξατε τὸν κονιορτὸν τῶν ποδῶν ὑμῶν.

With a preposition, the genitive often implies **"motion away from."** This basic meaning will also help to think of the three most important uses of the genitive.

SIMILARITIES

Many functions of the genitive in Greek are similar to the functions of "of" in English. You do not need to memorize these now (focus instead on memorizing **kind** and **separation**), but be aware of these more specific functions.

   a. **Possessive Genitive:** The house *of my father* (separating from all other houses).

b. **Genitive of source or material:** You are a letter *of Christ* (i.e., a letter *from Christ*).

c. **Partitive Genitive:** One *of the scribes* (separating from the rest).

If the noun qualified by the genitive is verbal (i.e., "the judgment"), the genitive may be **subjective** or **objective**. Like every aspect of grammar and syntax, these can only be determined in context.

d. **Subjective Genitive:** Who shall separate us from the love *of Christ*? (Rom 8.35) "Christ" is the subject of the verbal noun "love": i.e., "Who can separate us from the love with which Christ loves us?"

e. **Objective Genitive:** For the preaching *of the cross* is foolishness . . . (1 Cor 1:18) "Cross" is the object of the preaching, i.e., "For the preaching *about* the cross is foolishness . . ."

DIFFERENCES

The Greek genitive case also has different functions than the English "of" described above:

f. **Genitive of Time:** He came to Jesus *during the night* (John 3:2). Here, the genitive is used to express **time within which.**

g. **Genitive of Comparison**: You will see greater things *than these* (John 1:50). When a comparative is used (e.g., "greater"), in Greek look for the genitive for the reference of comparison ("than these").

h. **Genitive following Verbs of Sensing:** All who hear *his voice* (John 5:28). The implication may be that only part of his voice is heard (i.e., partitive genitive).

Genitive and Dative Cases

RECOGNIZING THE GENITIVE

A big help is that the genitive plural form *always* ends in -ῶν. Don't jump to the reverse conclusion, however, that every -ῶν is genitive plural! Some verb forms also have an -ῶν ending, so be sure to check the context and (as always) look for the article!

For singular forms of the genitive, look for the article as a guide, the -οῦ in masculine and neuter, and -ς in feminine.

INTRODUCTION: INDIRECT OBJECTS, "TO," AND "FOR"

The Indirect Object of a sentence in English usually occurs before the direct object and answers **to whom** or **for whom** the action of the verb takes place. This is most common in verbs of giving:

He gave to me the scroll.

The indirect object is "me" because it answers to whom he gave the scroll. Often we would omit the "to" in English and just say, "He gave me the scroll."

DEFINITION: THE DATIVE CASE

"To" and **"for"** are the keywords for translating the Greek dative case. However, this is only the tip of the iceberg of the uses of the dative in Greek. Besides the function of the indirect object (which is often translated "to" or "for"), it also has a **locative** function (denoting the place where or rest "**at**") and an **instrumental** function (the means by which an action was accomplished or an association with an action, often translated **"by"** or **"with"**).

You should learn these three functions generally as:

1. Dative of Interest: "to" or "for"

They promised to give to him the money. (Mark 14:11) (Indirect Object)
ἐπηγγείλαντο αὐτῷ ἀργύριον δοῦναι.

Do not be anxious for your life. (Matt 6:25) (Dative of Interest)
μὴ μεριμνᾶτε τῇ ψυχῇ ὑμῶν.

His name was John. (John 1:6) (Dative of Possession)
ὄνομα αὐτῷ Ἰωάννης. (literally, "a name to him was John.")

2. Locative Dative: "on," "at," or "in"

>...and put it <u>on his head.</u> (John 19:2) (Dative of Place Where)
>ἐπέθηκαν αὐτοῦ <u>τῇ κεφαλῇ</u>.

>...<u>on the third day</u> be raised. (Matt 16:21) (Dative of Time At)
><u>τῇ τρίτῃ ἡμέρᾳ</u> ἐγερθῆναι.

>Blessed are the poor <u>in spirit</u>... (Matt 5:3) (Dative of Sphere)
>μακάριοι οἱ πτωχοὶ <u>τῷ πνεύματι</u>...

3. Dative of Instrument or Association: "by" or "with"

>I partake <u>with thanks.</u> (1 Cor 10:30) (Dative of Manner)
>ἐγὼ <u>χάριτι</u> μετέχω.

>The chaff he will burn <u>with unquenchable fire.</u> (Matt 3:12) (Dative of Instrument)
>τὸ δὲ ἄχυρον κατακαύσει <u>πυρὶ ἀσβέστῳ</u>.

SIMILARITIES

The key words "to" and "for" have the closest function in English to the Greek dative. "To" and "for" will help in many cases: indirect object and datives of interest. It should be clear that this is a thin branch because "on," "at," "in," "by," or "with" may be more appropriate. As you read Greek, consider carefully how the dative functions in context.

DIFFERENCES

There is no good parallel between the Greek dative and the English language. The three basic functions of the dative and their keywords have to be memorized and tried in context.

RECOGNITION OF THE DATIVE

The dative is recognizable by the iota in all endings. In singular forms, the iota often occurs as a subscript below an alpha or eta. Be careful that you don't assume all iota subscripts are datives! Some verbal forms also use the iota-subscript. As always use the articles to help determine the case of the nouns.

Genitive and Dative Cases

EXERCISES

Identify how the underlined words function in the sentence using the categories described above (e.g., genitive of possession or dative of association).

1. The woman gave the Greek book <u>to the man</u>.

2. The book <u>of vocabulary</u> was heavier than he thought.

3. The <u>speech of Christ</u> stirred my heart.

4. Jesus went to Jerusalem <u>with his disciples</u>.

5. For <u>by grace</u> you have been saved through faith.
   Τῇ γὰρ <u>χάριτί</u> ἐστε σεσῳσμένοι διὰ πίστεως· (Eph 2:8)

6. He cried <u>in a loud voice</u> . . .
   <u>φωνῇ μεγάλῃ</u> ἐκραύγασεν . . . (John 11:43)

7. And they sent <u>to him their</u> disciples . . .
   καὶ ἀποστέλλουσιν <u>αὐτῷ</u> τοὺς μαθητὰς <u>αὐτῶν</u> . . . (Matt 22:16)

8. and getting a sponge, filling it <u>with sour wine</u> . . .
   λαβὼν σπόγγον πλήσας τε <u>ὄξους</u> . . . (Matt 27:48 Note genitive translated "with")

9. They went into the house <u>of Simon and Andrew</u> . . .
   ἦλθον εἰς τὴν οἰκίαν <u>Σίμωνος καὶ Ἀνδρέου</u> . . . (Mark 1:29)

10. Are you greater <u>than our father</u> Jacob?
    μὴ σὺ μείζων εἶ <u>τοῦ πατρὸς ἡμῶν</u> Ἰακώβ; (John 4:2; The indeclinable noun Ἰακώβ is also genitive. There are two more.)

6

Adjectives

DEVOTION

And four living creatures . . . chant "Holy, holy, holy, the Lord God the Almighty, who was and who is and who is coming." (Rev 4:8)

Καὶ τὰ τέσσαρα ζῷα λέγοντες· ἅγιος, ἅγιος, ἅγιος κύριος ὁ θεὸς ὁ παντοκράτωρ, ὁ ἦν καὶ ὁ ὢν καὶ ὁ ἐρχόμενος.

An adjective's main job is to describe something in greater detail. The book of Revelation loves adjectives and especially piles on adjectives describing God. The four living creatures around the throne recall Isaiah 6 when they chant "Holy, holy, holy"—using the adjective three times to emphasize the holiness of God, the radical otherness of God, that cannot be adequately described using human language.

Since all we have is human language, we try to describe God with more and more adjectives (especially omni- words): omnipresent, omniscient, omnipotent and so on. The book of Revelation describes God as holy, worthy, just, and true (for a few examples).

Some of these adjectives are also applied to Jesus: He is *worthy* to receive nouns like power, wealth, wisdom, might, honor, glory and blessing (5:12). Jesus is first introduced as "the faithful witness" (1:5), the prototype of the faithful witnesses who follow the Lamb.

We too will run out of words before we can describe God, but we can use as many as we have in any language to be faithful witnesses to the wondrous, awe-inspiring, magnificent, humbling grace of God through Jesus Christ.

DEFINITION: ADJECTIVE

An ***Adjective** is a word used with a noun or pronoun to describe, indicate, or count the number. Another way to detect an adjective is to put the word *very* in front of it (there are some exceptions!). Adjectives often answer the questions *What kind? How many? How much? Which? Whose? In what order?*

Adjectives

SIMILARITIES

Both Greek and English use adjectives in three ways: as attributive, predicate, or substantive.

1. Attributive: The attributive adjective describes an attribute or quality about the word it modifies. Often the attributive adjective limits the noun or pronoun by distinguishing it from other nouns.

You have kept the good wine until now. (John 2:10)

The wine is described as "good," which distinguishes it from other kinds of wine.

2. Predicate: When the adjective is in the *predicate position, it *asserts* something about the word it modifies. A key to recognizing the predicate is that some form of the verb "to be" is either stated or implied. Look for a form of "to be" and that the adjective is separated from the word it modifies. The focus is on asserting the quality of the noun or pronoun, and not on distinguishing it from others (as with attributive adjectives).

The man was blind.

The man is described as "blind," an adjective in the predicate following "was," a form of "to be." The sentence asserts some quality of the man.

3. Substantive: When an adjective is used like a noun, the quality is given "substance" and called *substantive. The key to recognizing the substantive is that it lacks a noun or pronoun modified by the adjective. The substantive adjective may have a definite article.

The wise will listen to God's word.

"Wise" does not modify any noun or pronoun and is preceded by the definite article "the"—so it is a substantive adjective.

DIFFERENCES

There are two main differences between English and Greek adjectives to keep in mind.

1. Greek adjectives change form based on gender as well as case and number (like the definite article). We learned that a Greek noun generally has only one gender (for example ὁ λόγος is always masculine). Attributive and predicate adjectives will match the noun they modify in gender and case and number. For example:

ὁ ἀγαθός λόγος
the good speech

ἀγαθός matches λόγος in case, number, and gender (note the endings). ἀγαθός is in a common attributive position, between the article and the noun.

ἡ γραφὴ ἡ ἀγαθή
the good writing

In this example, ἀγαθή matches γραφή in gender (feminine). In this case, the attributive adjective appears after the noun with a reduplication of the definite article. The key to recognizing this is to match the adjective to the noun by case, number and gender *and definiteness* (meaning if the noun has a definite article an attributive adjective should also have the definite article). Also note how it is translated into English.

The *lexical form of an adjective is the way you will find it if you look it up in a lexicon or in the back of your Greek textbook. *Turn to the lexicon in the back of your textbook (e.g., Croy p. 244 or Mounce p. 395) and note how adjectives appear.* Since adjectives will take the case of the noun they modify, they have three possible sets of endings. The nominative masculine ending is shown on the full entry and then only the ending is shown for the feminine and neuter (remember that this is grammatical gender and has no relationship to biological gender). For example:

ἀγαθός, -ή, -όν, good, noble

ἀγαθός is the masculine form; the feminine form will end with -ή (i.e., ἀγαθή); the neuter form will end with -όν (i.e., ἀγαθόν). Be sure to write your vocabulary cards this way to help you remember the different possible endings for an adjective.

2. **Placing a definite article in front of an adjective** without a matching noun makes it into a ***substantive** in Greek (functions like a noun). The key to recognizing the substantive is that no noun will match in case, number, and gender. When translating substantives, you may have to put in a word to clarify the gender. Masculine substantives may need "person" or "man"; feminine substantives may need "woman." A neuter substantive often will need "thing" or "things" to make sense in English.

ὁ ἀγαθός ἐστίν ...
The good *man* is ...

ἡ ἀγαθή ἐστίν ...
The good *woman* is ...

τὸ ἀγαθόν ἐστίν ...
The good *thing* is ...

Adjectives

EXERCISES

Circle the adjective(s). Write above whether the adjective is attributive, predicate, or substantive. If attributive or predicate, draw an arrow from the adjective to the noun it modifies in the following sentences.

1. A large crowd kept following him.

2. The well is deep.

3. There is a boy who has five loaves and two fish.

4. He cried with a loud voice, "Lazarus, come out!"

5. Now a man was ill.

6. The true light was coming into the world. (John 2:12)
   Ἦν τὸ φῶς τὸ ἀληθινόν ἐρχόμενον εἰς τὸν κόσμον.

7. I am not worthy to untie the thong of his sandal. (John 1:27)
   οὐκ εἰμί ἐγὼ ἄξιος ἵνα λύσω αὐτοῦ τὸν ἱμάντα τοῦ ὑποδήματος.

8. I will raise them up on the last day . . . (John 6:39)
   ἀναστήσω αὐτοὺς ἐν τῇ ἐσχάτῃ ἡμέρᾳ . . .

9. And another sign was seen in heaven: behold! A great red dragon! (Rev 12:3)
   καὶ ὤφθη ἄλλο σημεῖον ἐν τῷ οὐρανῷ, καὶ ἰδοὺ δράκων μέγας πυρρὸς.

10. Five of them were foolish and five were wise . . . (Matt 25:2)
    πέντε δὲ ἐξ αὐτῶν ἦσαν μωραὶ καὶ πέντε φρόνιμοι . . .

7

Prepositions—Fine Tuning Relationships

DEVOTION

. . . for the words that you gave to me I have given to them, and they have received them and know in truth that I came from you; and they have believed that you sent me. (NRSV John 17:8)

ὅτι τὰ ῥήματα ἃ ἔδωκάς μοι δέδωκα αὐτοῖς, καὶ αὐτοὶ ἔλαβον καὶ ἔγνωσαν ἀληθῶς ὅτι παρὰ σοῦ ἐξῆλθον, καὶ ἐπίστευσαν ὅτι σύ με ἀπέστειλας.

The Gospel of John is insistent and focused on answering the questions: From where did Jesus come? Who sent Jesus? Jesus answers these questions in various ways, including calling God "the-One-Who-Sent-Me" (John 7:28; 8:26; 8:29; 13:16). God sent Jesus. Jesus' words and deeds have their origin and authority from God.

In the above verse from chapter 17, John describes why Jesus' origin is so crucial in the stages of faith: first, Jesus' words are given; next, a person receives them. Belief, however, is not equated with reception but in knowing and acting on the truth that the Father sent Jesus, that (in the words of the NRSV) Jesus came *from* the Father.

There are many prepositions in Greek that could be translated "from." One would imply that Jesus came from inside the father (ἐκ). Another would indicate he came from outside the Father (ἀπὸ). The preposition used, however, suggests that Jesus was *beside* the father (παρά), so "I came from *beside* you." This may suggest the kind of "sitting at the right hand of the Father" image that is used in the letter to the Hebrews (Heb 1:3) and the book of Revelation (Rev 3:21). If a spatial metaphor is appropriate for describing the Son's relationship with the Father, it is "sitting besides," or in the words of the Athanasian Creed, "equal in glory, coeternal in majesty."

For Christians, this is incredible good news: Jesus comes to us as one who is "beside" the Father—and thus can bring us all we need that only God can provide: salvation, healing, forgiveness, justice; in other words, God's very kingdom. As we study Greek, this Jesus assures us that our relationship with God is secure because we know "the One who sent him."

Prepositions—Fine Tuning Relationships

DEFINITION: PREPOSITION

A ***Preposition** is a word that indicates the relationship between two *nouns (or noun equivalents such as a *substantive). For example:

> *Jesus answered [Nathanael],*
> *"I saw you <u>under</u> the fig tree before Philip called you." (John 1:48)*

The word "under" clarifies the relationship between Nathanael ("you") and the "fig tree"—he was under it. The word following the preposition is called the **object of the preposition**. In this case, "the fig tree" is the object of the preposition "under." The preposition together with its object (with all its modifiers, in this example, "a" and "fig") is called a *prepositional phrase. Varying the preposition would vary the meaning, for example: "I saw you <u>in</u> the fig tree" uses "in" to place Nathanael in the tree (he would be like Zaccheus!).

Many prepositions help describe the relationship between two words in space. For this reason, we say that prepositions are primarily **spatial**. Consider the spatial qualities of the following:

in	on	under	over
through	down	among	around
upon	beside	near	with

Note how these spatial prepositions can also be used **qualitatively**. For example,

> *. . . the ruler of this world is coming. He has no power <u>over</u> me. (John 14:30)*

"Me" is the object of the preposition "over." The relationship between "power" and "me" is not one of space but of quality. In other words, Jesus is not influenced by the power of the ruler of this world. However, the phrase retains some of the spatial sense by evoking a picture of the ruler of this world above Jesus, perhaps with Jesus wagging his finger "no."

Although many of these prepositions have a spatial meaning, some also indicate the **manner** or the **instrument** of the action. Consider:

> *. . . a child, a male son, who will rule the nations <u>with</u> a rod of iron. (Rev 12:5)*

"With" does not simply indicate a spatial relationship of a rod next to a child, but that the rod is the instrument of ruling. "A rod of iron" is the object of the preposition "with."

BRUSHING UP ENGLISH TO LEARN GREEK

SIMILARITIES

Both Greek and English use prepositions to relate two *nouns (or equivalents), and both generally position the preposition in front of its object. Both Greek and English place that object in an objective (or oblique) case. For example, "him" is the objective case of "he" in English, so we would say "Jesus has power <u>over him</u>" (not "Jesus has power over he"). Both Greek and English use prepositions to indicate spatial, qualitative, and instrumental relationships. Neither Greek nor English inflects prepositions (meaning they never change form).

DIFFERENCES

If this all sounds familiar to our discussion about the genitive and dative, it should. Differently than English, prepositions in Greek began life as adverbs used to clarify the function of the case. By the time the New Testament was written, however, prepositions had taken over much of the work that cases used to do.

Despite the increased role of the prepositions at the time of the New Testament, it is still better (and easier) first to consider the sense of the case and then to add the root meaning of the preposition. Think of it like a telescope that has a gross adjustment and a fine adjustment. When viewing a star, an astronomer first adjusts the gross wheel to get a general focus on the object. Then, she switches to the fine knob to sharpen the view of the star. Likewise, let the case determine the possibilities of meaning generally and then use the preposition to fine tune the meaning within the context of the sentence. Thus we can say that a preposition "fine tunes" the case.

In the last chapters, we talked about the base meanings of the case. Now, with the addition of the accusative, it is repeated to memorize with prepositions.[1]

With a preposition, the
    accusative case denotes   extension, or **motion towards**,
    genitive case denotes   separation or **motion from**, and
    dative case denotes   the place where, or **rest at** (locative)
        or   the **means** by which an action is accomplished
        or   **association** (also instrumental).

Memorizing these base meanings of the cases will help make sense of the various meanings of prepositions below.

ROOT MEANINGS OF PREPOSITIONS

Each of these should be memorized; a guideword is given to help remember these root meanings.[2]

---

1. Nunn. *Short Syntax*, 28.
2. See Nunn, *Short Syntax*, 30–31; Croy, *Primer*, 29–30; Mounce, *BBG*, 339.

Prepositions—Fine Tuning Relationships

Prepositions connected with Accusative only:

ἀνά	**Up**	"anabasis" = marching UP (also Again, "anabaptism" = baptized AGAIN)
εἰς	**Into** (to the interior)	"eisegesis" = reading a meaning INTO a text

Prepositions connected with the Genitive only

ἀντί	**Over Against**	"antichrist" = AGAINST Christ
ἀπό	**Away From** (from the exterior)	"apostasy" = standing AWAY FROM the truth
ἐκ	**Out Of** (from the interior)	"ecstasy" = standing OUT OF oneself
πρό	**In Front Of**	"prologue" = IN FRONT OF the story

Prepositions connected with the Dative only

ἐν	**In** (also With)	"in"
σύν	**Together With**	"symphony" = sounding TOGETHER WITH others

Prepositions connected with the Accusative and Genitive

διά	**Through**	"diameter" = the path THROUGH a circle
κατά	**Down**	"catalogue" = list DOWN
μετά	**Among**	"metaphor" = carries a concept AMONG another concept
περί	**Around**	"perimeter" = the path AROUND a shape
ὑπέρ	**Over**	"hyperactive" = OVER-active
ὑπό	**Under**	"hypodermic" = UNDER the dermis (layer of skin)

Prepositions connected with the Accusative, Genitive and Dative

ἐπί	**Upon**	"epidermis" = UPON the dermis
παρά	**Beside**	"parallel" = a line BESIDE another line
πρός	**Towards**	"proselyte" = a person who comes TOWARDS a religion

EXAMPLES

1. The root meaning of παρά is BESIDE. With the accusative case, which has the basic meaning of **motion towards**, it denotes *motion alongside*:

> *And as he sowed, some fell <u>alongside the road.</u> (Matt 13:4)*
> καὶ ἐν τῷ σπείρειν αὐτὸν ἃ μὲν ἔπεσεν <u>παρὰ τὴν ὁδόν</u>.

2. With the genitive, which has the basic meaning of **motion from**, παρά denotes *motion from beside*:

> *they know truly that I come <u>from beside you.</u> (John 17:8)*
> ἔγνωσαν ἀληθῶς ὅτι <u>παρὰ σοῦ</u> ἐξῆλθον.

3. With the dative, which has the basic meaning of **rest (locative)**, then παρά denotes *rest besides*.

> *Jesus . . . taking a child placed it <u>near himself</u>. (Luke 9:47)*
> ὁ δὲ Ἰησοῦς . . . ἐπιλαβόμενος παιδίον ἔστησεν αὐτὸ <u>παρ' ἑαυτῷ</u>.

4. ἐν always is followed by the dative, and often indicates the locative (**in**) or instrumental (**with** or **by**). The New Testament especially uses ἐν with the instrumental meaning, as in this example:

> *Lord, shall we strike <u>with the sword</u>? (Luke 22:49)*
> κύριε, εἰ πατάξομεν <u>ἐν μαχαίρῃ</u>;

Another difference from English is the use of prepositions as prefixes of verbs. This is very common and one of the reasons for memorizing the basic meanings of prepositions. A verb prefixed in this way often will take objects in cases that fit with the preposition. Also, **augments and reduplication of verb stems happen after any prepositional prefix**. This is another reason that prepositions need to be memorized now. When we get to verbs, we'll need to be able to identify these prefixes in order to identify the stem. For example:

ἀναβαίν-ω	<u>ἀνα</u>-βαίν-ω	I walk <u>up</u>
ἀπέρχ-ομαι	<u>ἀπο</u>-έρχ-ομαι	I go <u>away</u>
διέρχ-ομαι	<u>δια</u>-έρχ-ομαι	I go <u>through</u>
εἰσέρχ-ομαι	<u>εἰσ</u>-έρχ-ομαι	I go <u>into</u>

Sometimes the prefix will be repeated as a preposition, which may be part of the Koine dialect's penchant for clarification, but also may be for emphasis. For example,

> *. . . and you have entered <u>into their labor</u>. (John 4:38)*
> . . . καὶ ὑμεῖς <u>εἰς τὸν κόπον</u> αὐτῶν <u>εἰσεληλύθατε</u>.

PREPOSITIONS—*FINE TUNING RELATIONSHIPS*

As the translator, you will have to decide whether this repetition is significant or not, and how to express it in English (if at all).

EXERCISES

Circle the preposition(s) and underline the prepositional phrase(s) in the following sentences.

1. I fell asleep on my book.

2. I took my Greek flash cards with me.

3. The student is climbing up a steep hill.

4. The jogger ran around the block and fell down on the ground in exhaustion.

5. The coat that his father had put over his head was torn and thrown out of reach.

6. There was a wedding in Cana of Galilee. (John 2:1a)
   γάμος ἐγένετο ἐν Κανὰ τῆς Γαλιλαίας.

7. And the Word was with God. (John 1:1b)
   καὶ ὁ λόγος ἦν πρὸς τὸν θεόν.

8. After this he went down to Capernaum. (John 2:12)
   Μετὰ τοῦτο κατέβη εἰς Καφαρναοὺμ αὐτὸς.

9. And he spent some time there with them. (John 3:22)
   καὶ ἐκεῖ διέτριβεν μετ' αὐτῶν.

10. Before Philip called you, I saw you under the fig tree. (John 1:48)
    πρὸ τοῦ σε Φίλιππον φωνῆσαι ὄντα ὑπὸ τὴν συκῆν εἶδόν σε.

8

Pronouns—Standing in for Nouns

DEVOTION

Jesus says to them, "I am the way, the truth and the life." (John 14:6).

λέγει αὐτῷ ὁ Ἰησοῦς, ἐγώ εἰμι ἡ ὁδὸς καὶ ἡ ἀλήθεια καὶ ἡ ζωή.

A pronoun is a word that stands in for a noun. Perhaps the most famous pronoun is "I" in Jesus' "I am" (ἐγώ εἰμι) sayings in the gospel according to John. Consider a brief sample:

- "I am the bread of life" (John 4:35, 51).
- "I am the light of the world" (John 8:12; 9:5).
- "Unless you come to believe that I AM, you will surely die in your sins" (John 8:24).
- "When you lift up the Son of Man, then you will realize that I AM" (John 8:28).
- "Before Abraham even came into existence, I AM" (John 8:58).

The word "I" refers to "Jesus." In the first two examples, Jesus uses the pronoun to assert something about himself (notice the predicate nominative). In the last three examples, there is no predicate. Instead, Jesus is using this formula to remind his hearers of God's name given in Exodus 3. Moses asks, "What name shall I say to them?" and God responds, "Thus you shall say to the Israelites, 'I AM has sent me to you.'" God's name in Hebrew is spelled YHWH (also called the Tetragrammaton for "four letters"), which are the same consonants for the Hebrew word "I AM."

In John, Jesus is presented as speaking in the same way as YHWH, "I AM." This is good news for us. When Jesus offers forgiveness, life and salvation in his name, he is speaking as fully divine. God's promises through Jesus can be trusted because he is I AM. We can know God through Jesus because he is I AM.[1]

---

1. For further reading, see Brown, *The Gospel According to John I–XII*, 533–538.

Pronouns—Standing in for Nouns

DEFINITION: PRONOUN

A ***Pronoun** is a word that stands in for a noun. It matches the number and gender of the noun it replaces. We are going to focus on personal pronouns here ("I," "you," "him/her/it," "they," etc.) and leave the rest for later.

SIMILARITIES

Both Greek and English use pronouns in the place of nouns.

Jesus walked by the sea. He saw Peter and Andrew.

"He" stands in for "Jesus" in the second sentence. We say "Jesus" is the ***antecedent** of "he."
You can replace "he" with "Jesus" and have the same meaning:

Jesus walked by the sea. Jesus saw Peter and Andrew.

This example helps us see why we use pronouns: to avoid being repetitious and awkward.

In both languages the number of the pronoun corresponds with the *number and *gender of the noun it replaces. (Remember that English has "natural gender" and Greek does not.) "He" matches the gender and number of "Jesus" (masculine, singular).

In both languages the *case depends on how the pronoun functions in its sentence, **not how the *antecedent functioned in its sentence.** The case of the pronoun and its antecedent noun are independent!

Jesus walked by the sea.
He saw Peter and Andrew.
Peter and Andrew saw him.

In the second sentence, "he" is the subject, thus is in the subjective case. In the third sentence, the pronoun is the direct object; the objective form in English is "him."

For an even better sounding sentence, we can replace "Peter and Andrew" with the pronoun "they" (plural):

They saw him.

In English and Greek, context is necessary to understand what is being said. If this sentence stood alone, we would have no idea who saw whom. But in the context of the previous sentences, we infer that "they" means "Peter and Andrew" and "him" means "Jesus." When there is ambiguity, it is interesting to think through all the possibilities.

In both English and Greek, we talk about which *person a pronoun is. The *person of a pronoun indicates the relationship with the speaker or audience. There are three classes of persons:

1st person "I" or "we" (the speaker refers to her- or himself, singular or plural)
2nd person "you" (the speaker refers to the audience, singular or plural)
3rd person "she," "he," "it" (singular) or "they" (plural) (the speaker refers to someone or something other than self or audience)

When parsing a pronoun, always be sure to give its *person.

DIFFERENCES

There are four differences to think about. The last one is the most complex (Mounce devotes chapter 12 of *BBG* to the subject).

1. **1st and 2nd person Greek pronouns may indicate emphasis.** Since the ending of verbs indicates 1st or 2nd person, singular or plural, a pronoun is not necessary. As a translator you will have to decide if it functions to emphasize the subject. If the verb is omitted, then the pronoun may be necessary.

2. **Basic Greek case meanings should be applied to pronouns.** For example, when you see a genitive pronoun, start to go through the basic meanings (kind and separation) and see if adding "of" makes sense. For dative pronouns, look at the context to see if it is a dative of interest, location, or instrument and if an English word needs to be added to make sense. Do not assume you will need to add an English word, especially following a preposition.

3. **The plural forms of 1st and 2nd person pronouns can be remembered** by thinking of the rough breathing with eta for "we/us" and the rough breathing with upsilon for "you."

4. **The third person pronouns αὐτός, αὐτή, αὐτό (he, she, it) can also function as adjectives.** We won't go into detail here. Right now, prepare yourself to stop and think carefully when you see αὐτός: is it acting like a personal pronoun (standing in for a noun) or is it acting like an adjective?

Pronouns—Standing in for Nouns

EXERCISES

Circle the pronoun(s) in John 2 (the Wedding of Cana). Write its person (1st, 2nd or 3rd) next to the circle. If the noun that it is replacing is in context (including other sentences), draw an arrow to it from the pronoun.

1. Jesus and his disciples had been invited to the wedding.

2. And the mother of Jesus said to him, "They have no wine."

3. And Jesus said to her, "Woman, what concern is that to you and to me?"

4. "My hour has not yet come."

5. His mother said to the servants:

6. "Do whatever he tells you."

7. Jesus said to them, "Fill the jars with water."

8. And they filled them up to the brim.

9. When the steward tasted the water, he did not know where it came from.

10. The steward called the bridegroom and said to him, "Everyone serves good wine first."

9

Passive Voice

DEVOTION

And just as Moses lifted up the serpent in the wilderness, in the same way the son of humanity must be lifted up. (John 3:14)

Καὶ καθὼς Μωϋσῆς ὕψωσεν τὸν ὄφιν ἐν τῇ ἐρήμῳ, οὕτως ὑψωθῆναι δεῖ τὸν υἱὸν τοῦ ἀνθρώπου.

In the first half of this sentence, Moses is the one who lifts up the serpent in the wilderness, reminding us of the episode in Numbers 21. The people of Israel had become impatient and complained against God and Moses, ungrateful for liberation from Egypt and the food provided on the way. "Why have you brought us up out of Egypt to die in the wilderness? For there is no food and no water, and we detest this miserable food" (Num 21:5). God sent poisonous snakes, and the people confessed their sins to God. God told Moses to set up a bronze serpent in the middle of the camp so that everyone who looked at it will live.

    In John's gospel, Jesus presents himself like the bronze serpent, as one who is lifted up. He uses the passive voice to emphasize this connection—and to obscure who will lift him up and what that will look like. By using the passive voice to suggest this ambiguity, John creates two levels of meaning. To every eye, Jesus will be lifted up on a cross by Roman centurions. To the eyes of faith, John makes the connection with the bronze serpent to suggest that, on a deeper level, Jesus will be lifted up so that everyone who looks at him and believes in him will live. To the eyes of faith, God is the agent who lifts Jesus up on the cross so that we will live.

DEFINITION: PASSIVE VOICE

The ***Passive Voice** indicates that the grammatical subject of the verb is the *receiver of the action (what is acted upon) and not the *agent (the doer of the action). For example, take the sentence "The Son is sent by the Father":

Passive Voice

	subject	*verb*	*prep. phrase*
Passive voice:	The Son	is sent	by the Father.
	receiver	verb	agent

We can re-write the passive voice into the active voice by making the *agent the grammatical subject of the verb:

	subject	*verb*	*object*
Active voice:	The Father	sent	the Son
	agent	verb	receiver

SIMILARITIES

1. The purpose of the passive voice is to emphasize what is being acted upon, i.e., the *receiver rather than the agent. For example, the sentence "The Son is sent by the Father" emphasizes the identity of the Son.

2. Both Greek and English use a preposition to explicitly state the agent. In English we use the preposition "by"; in Greek ὑπό.

> *They are being baptized <u>by John</u> in the Jordan River.*
> βαπτίζονται <u>ὑπ᾽ Ἰωάννου</u> ἐν τῷ Ἰορδάνῃ ποταμῷ.

The grammatical subject of the sentence is "they," and they are the ones being acted upon ("baptized"). The agent (the one who is baptizing) is explicitly expressed in the prepositional phrase. John is the agent who is baptizing. We can re-write this sentence:

> *<u>John</u> is baptizing them in the Jordan River.*
> <u>Ἰωάννης</u> βαπτίζει αὐτούς ἐν τῷ Ἰορδάνῃ ποταμῷ.

3. Sometimes the agent is omitted. As a reader, you have to decide if the agent is important or not. In some cases, it is impossible to determine the agent and to focus on the agent is to miss the emphasis on the receiver. For example (the passive verb is underlined):

> *<u>Are</u> not two sparrows <u>sold</u> for a penny?*
> οὐχὶ δύο στρουθία ἀσσαρίου πωλεῖται;

It doesn't really matter who is selling the sparrows. The emphasis is on the sparrows and their price.

4. Other times, you will be able to infer the agent from context. In many cases, God will be the implied agent. This is called the ***divine passive**. As a result of Jewish piety that became Christian piety, New Testament authors sometimes use the passive voice to avoid (mis)using the name of God. The use of the passive voice can also suggest ambiguity about the agent, which makes it more exegetically interesting. For example, when Jesus speaks these words is he forgiving the paralytic or is God? (Look at the context of the verse for more information.)

Child, your sins are forgiven. (Mark 2:5)
τέκνον, ἀφίεωταί σου αἱ ἁμαρτίαι.

DIFFERENCES

1. Greek changes the form of the verb to reflect the passive voice. English uses forms of "be" with past participles (often ending in "-ed"). The Greek endings (e.g., Croy p. 48; Mounce p. 150) must be memorized in order to recognize the passive voice.

2. In Greek, the forms of the continuous passive and middle are identical and can only be distinguished in context (which is why we call them "middle/passive endings"). We will look at the middle voice in the next chapter.

3. In Greek, some verbs are middle/passive in *form* but active in *meaning*. These verbs are called ***deponents** and they are important enough to mention here and again in the next chapter. The three most important of these are γίν-ομαι (I become), ἔρχ-ομαι (I come, go) and δύνα-μαι (I am able)[1]. Two things can help you remember *deponents: (1) if the verb ends with -ομαι on your vocabulary cards (i.e., the lexical form), then it is *deponent. (2) When you parse one of these verbs, write "deponent" as its voice (even though technically it is not a voice). This practice may help you remember which verbs are *deponent.

EXERCISES

Rewrite the following sentences, changing verbs from *active voice* to *passive voice*. Be sure to keep the time of the verb the same.

1. God will wipe away every tear.

2. Jesus healed the man.

3. The disciples threw the net on the other side of the boat.

1. Note that δύνα-μαι is irregular.

Passive Voice

4. Lydia provided a place for Paul to rest.

5. After taking bread, he broke it.

Rewrite the following sentences, changing verbs from the *passive voice* to *active voice*. For some examples, you will have to infer God or another as the agent. Be sure that you keep the time of the verb the same.

6. He was baptized in the river by John.

7. The man's sins were forgiven by Jesus.

8. Paul was sent by the Holy Spirit to Macedonia.

9. They were given white robes.

10. They will be called children of God.

10

Middle Voice

DEVOTION

I advise you to buy from me
>   gold refined by fire so that you may become rich, and
>   white garments so that you may clothe yourself
>   and the shame of your nakedness will not be revealed, and
>   ointment to anoint your eyes so that you may see. (Rev 3:18)

συμβουλεύω σοι ἀγοράσαι παρ' ἐμοῦ
>   χρυσίον πεπυρωμένον ἐκ πυρὸς ἵνα πλουτήσῃς, καὶ
>   ἱμάτια λευκὰ ἵνα περιβάλῃ
>   καὶ μὴ φανερωθῇ ἡ αἰσχύνη τῆς γυμνότητός σου, καὶ
>   κολλούριον ἐγχρῖσαι τοὺς ὀφθαλμούς σου ἵνα βλέπῃς.

The Christian community in Laodicea has become spiritually and socially self-satisfied. They say, "I am rich! I have prospered! I have no needs!" (3:17). Through the prophet John, Jesus tells them they are buying the wrong products from the wrong vendor. The kind of "gold" they should buy comes from him not from trade with Babylon (18:16). Gold paves the streets of the New Jerusalem (21:21)—they should desire to enter there!

White robes symbolize God's servants—the twenty-four elders around the throne (4:4), the martyrs under the throne (6:11), the saints washed by the blood of the Lamb (7:13–14), and the righteous deeds of the saints (19:8). Ointment for the eyes helps them to see. Revelation is all about seeing: revealing the cosmic realities behind the day-to-day life in the Roman Empire.

The phrase translated "clothe yourself" is a translation of a verb in the middle voice, περιβάλῃ. The middle voice indicates that the agent is in some way also the receiver of the action; in this case, the Laodiceans are both acting (putting on clothes) and receiving (the clothes go on their bodies). Throughout the book of Revelation, John invites Christians to act like God's servants, to wear God's clothes. They can't be self-satisfied when God is the one who gave them robes to clothe themselves!

MIDDLE VOICE

DEFINITION: MIDDLE VOICE

The true *Middle Voice indicates that the grammatical subject of the verb is *both* the *agent (the doer of the action) and in some way the *receiver of the action (what is acted upon). The true middle is rare in NT Greek, as we will discuss below, but common enough to require mention. The key word when translating the true middle is the English reflexive pronoun "self."

SIMILARITIES

In English, we use some form of "self" with verbs to express that a person's actions affect oneself. ("Myself," "himself," "herself," and "themselves" are called *reflexive pronouns because they reflect back on the subject.) For example, we express the idea of the middle voice in the English sentences "I shaved *myself*" and "They kept money *for themselves*." These are the two main ways that the *subject is also the *receiver.

1.   **Direct Middle.** In this case, the middle voice indicates that the *subject of the verb is both *agent and direct object. For example, consider the sentence "I shaved," which implies the expanded form "I shaved *myself*":

	subject	verb	direct object
Middle voice:	I	shaved	myself.
	agent	verb	receiver

The subject ("I") acts ("shaved") and is also the recipient of the action. "Myself" is implied in the sentence, but sometimes will be stated for clarity or emphasis. Compare:

	subject	verb	direct object
Active voice:	I	shaved	Paul.
	agent	verb	receiver

	subject	verb	prepositional phrase
Passive voice:	Paul	was shaved	by me.
	receiver	verb	agent

In Greek, the reflexive quality may be expressed through the middle voice of the verb form. For example, the English sentence "I wash myself" would be communicated by one word in Greek: λούομαι.

In the example "I shaved myself," "myself" is redundant. Likewise, in Greek the reflexive pronoun may be used redundantly with the middle voice. As with English, the redundant reflexive pronoun may clarify the middle voice or emphasize the reflexive quality in a particular context. For example, James 1:22 uses the reflexive pronoun ἑαυτούς even when not necessary, but it makes clear that hearers who don't act on the word are deluding only themselves and not God or someone else.

*But prove yourselves doers of the word,
and not merely hearers who <u>delude themselves</u>. (James 1:22)*
γίνεσθε δὲ ποιηταὶ λόγου
καὶ μὴ μόνον ἀκροαταὶ <u>παραλογιζόμενοι ἑαυτούς</u>.

2.   **Indirect Middle.** In this case, the middle voice indicates that the *subject of the verb is both *agent and the *indirect object; the subject is acting for (or against) his/her own interest or advantage/disadvantage. For example, examine the sentence "They kept some money for themselves":

	subject	verb	direct object	indirect object
Middle voice:	They	kept	money	for themselves.
	agent	verb		recipient

In Greek the middle voice of the verb expresses what in English requires the phrase "for themselves," as in Acts 5:2 below. The one Greek word ἐνοσφίσατο requires the five words in English to express the idea of the middle voice.

<u>ἐνοσφίσατο</u> ἀπὸ τῆς τιμῆς
<u>He kept back</u> some of the price <u>for himself</u> (Acts 5:2).

The dative case of the reflexive pronoun could also express this idea (see chapter 5 on the dative of interest).

3.   **Deponent Middle.** In Greek, some common verbs are middle in *form* but active in *meaning*. These verbs are called *deponents. There is no active or passive form of an aspect stem that is deponent.[1] Perhaps the closest English has to the Greek *deponent is verbs that are classified as active voice but the action reflects back on the grammatical subject and they cannot be transformed into the passive voice with the same meaning or cannot take a different indirect object than the subject. Consider,

The jar <u>contains</u> pickles.

We could re-write the sentence as:

The jar <u>contains in itself</u> pickles.

The verb "contains" reflects back on the subject (the jar also receives the action); we can't make it passive ("pickles are contained by the jar" communicates something different).

1. See below. Although deponent in one stem, it may be active in another!

MIDDLE VOICE

The politician <u>lacks</u> wisdom.

We could re-write this sentence as:

The politician <u>lacks</u> wisdom <u>for himself</u>.

The verb "lacks" reflects back on the subject (to the disadvantage of the politician!); we can't make it passive ("Wisdom is lacked by the politician" doesn't make sense); and we can't use a different indirect object.

These, however, are only rough equivalents to the Greek *deponent to help remember that the deponent is **middle/passive in form and active in meaning**.

RECOGNITION

1. In Greek, the forms of the continuous passive and middle are identical and can only be distinguished in context (which is why we call them "middle/passive endings"). The primary endings are shown below with connecting vowels separated by a dash:

	Singular	Plural
1st	-ο-μαι	-ο-μεθα
2nd	-η²	-ε-σθε
3rd	-ε-ται	-ο-νται

When you see these endings, think "This verb is middle or passive. Which one?" To decide whether a particular form is middle or passive in context:

> a. **Look at the lexical form.** If the lexical form of the verb ends in -ομαι, then it is *deponent (see below for common forms). Many of the verbs with middle/passive endings that you will see in introductory NT Greek will be *deponent and when you parse them you should write "deponent" as the voice (even though it is not technically a voice).
>
> πορεύ<u>ονται</u> εἰς Καφαρναούμ.
>
> The lexical form of πορεύονται is πορεύ-ομαι (I travel). The -ομαι ending indicates it is deponent in the Continous stem. Parse πορεύονται as Continous, <u>Deponent</u>, Indicative, Present, Third Person, Plural; lexical form πορεύ-ομαι.
>
> So, you would translate:

2. The uncontracted second person plural middle/passive ending is -σαι, but since the Greek ear doesn't like the s sound between vowels, it is contracted when used with a connecting vowel.

They are traveling into Capernaum.

b. **Look for a prepositional phrase with ὑπό.** If the object of ὑπό is the agent of the verb, then the ending is passive (see the previous chapter).

βαπτίζεται εἰς τὸν Ἰορδάνην ὑπὸ Ἰωάννου.

The lexical form of βαπτίζεται is βαπτίζ-ω (I baptize), which does not end in -ομαι, so it is not deponent but either a true middle or a passive. So, look for the preposition ὑπό. And there it is: ὑπὸ Ἰωάννου. This expresses that John is the agent doing the baptizing. You parse βαπτίζεται as Continuous, Passive, Indicative, Present, Third Person, Singular; lexical form βαπτίζ-ω and translate:

He is baptized in the Jordan by John.

c. **Try the Passive first.** The true middle is rare, and so it is more likely to be passive. If you've eliminated the deponent as a possibility and there is no prepositional phrase with ὑπό, then try the passive to see if it makes sense.

ἡμεῖς διδασκόμεθα.

The lexical form of διδασκόμεθα is διδάσκ-ω (I teach), so it is not deponent. There is no preposition ὑπό. It is probably best to take it as a passive without stated agent:

We are being taught.

As discussed in the last chapter, this could be a *divine passive:

We are being taught (by God).

Or the agent may be clear from another sentence in context:

We are being taught (by Paul, Mary, etc.).

d. **Last, try the true middle.** When you've exhausted other options, and nothing seems to fit the context, try the middle voice using a form of *self* in your translation:

ἡμεῖς διδασκόμεθα.

in the right context may be translated:

We are teaching <u>ourselves</u>. (direct middle)

MIDDLE VOICE

or

We are teaching <u>for ourselves</u>. (indirect middle; i.e., "for the benefit of ourselves")

2. Remember: The true middle is rare in the New Testament. ***Deponents are very common!**

3. To remember deponents:
   a. Memorize the most common *deponent verbs in the continuous stem:

ἀποκρίν-ομαι	I answer
βούλ-ομαι	I wish
γίν-ομαι	I become
δύνα-μαι	I am able
ἔρχ-ομαι	I go/come
πορεύ-ομαι	I travel

   b. Write verbs on your Greek vocabulary cards with a dash between the continuous stem and the ending. When you see -ομαι on your vocabulary cards, in the lexicon or in the back of your Greek textbook, think "Oh, my! It's deponent!"

   c. Train yourself to write "deponent" for voice when parsing.

4. **Some verbs will be deponent in one stem but not another.** The two most important right now are:
   a. ἔρχ-ομαι (I go/come) which is deponent in the continuous stem, but is active in both form and meaning in the Aorist stem (Aorist stem is ἐλθ-; principle part is ἦλθ-ον) and

   b. εἰμί (I am) which is deponent in the future (ἔσ-ομαι). (E.g., Croy p. 67 or Mounce p. 163.)

These simply have to be memorized!

5. Some verbs will have **one meaning in the active voice and a completely different meaning in the middle voice.** The most important of these are:

Active Voice:	ἄρχ-ω (I rule)
Middle Voice:	ἄρχ-ομαι (I begin)
Active Voice:	ἅπτ-ω (I light, kindle)
Middle Voice:	ἅπτ-ομαι (I touch)

EXERCISES

Although the purpose of this book is to brush up English skills, it is crucial that you be able to identify deponent verbs and translate them as active. **Practice translating the following Greek deponent verbs as active.** Some verbs have prepositional prefixes; separate the prefix first to see the verbal stem and then translate. These are all continuous present—**so make sure you emphasize the continuous aspect!**

    Example: ἐξέρχονται

Separate prepositional prefix: ἐκ[3] + ερχονται (from ἔρχ-ομαι)
Separate ending from stem: ἐκ + ερχ + ονται
Parse: Continuous <u>Deponent</u> Indicative Present Third Person Plural; lexical form ἐξέρχ-ομαι
Translate: They are coming/going out

1. ἔρχεται

2. δύνανται

3. γίνεται

4. διερχόμεθα

5. εἰσέρχονται

6. ἀποκρίνεσθε

7. πορεύομαι

8. ἄρχεσθε

9. ἐκπορεύομαι

    [3]. ἐκ changes to ἐξ when followed by a vowel.

Middle Voice

10. βούλεται

Rewrite the following sentences into an equivalent of the middle voice by removing the direct object or indirect object and replacing it with a form of self **that reflects back on the subject.**

> *Example:* He clothed the servants.
> *Re-write as:* He clothed himself.
>
> *Example:* They gave for others. (i.e., "for the benefit of others")
> *Re-write as:* They gave for themselves.

11. She washed her children.

12. They taught the disciples the word of the Lord.

13. Mary chose the best for Martha (i.e., "for Martha's benefit").

14. You received the truth for them (i.e., "for their benefit")

15. They will be called children of God.

11

Continuous Past

DEVOTION

And going forward a little, he fell on the ground and kept on praying that, if it was possible, the hour may pass from him. (Mark 14:35)

καὶ προελθὼν μικρὸν ἔπιπτεν ἐπὶ τῆς γῆς καὶ προσηύχετο ἵνα εἰ δυνατόν ἐστιν παρέλθῃ ἀπ' αὐτοῦ ἡ ὥρα.

When Jesus prays in the garden of Gethsemane, Mark uses the continuous past προσηύχετο (προς + ε + εὐχ + ετο) to describe this action. It suggests that the short prayer in the next verse was not prayed simply once, but again and again in past time. "Abba, Father, for you all things are possible, remove this cup from me; yet, not what I want, but what you want." Jesus is so persistent in his prayer and that persistence communicates something of Jesus' humanity, freedom, and trust. He is so human in his desire to avoid the shame and suffering of the cross. He is free to ask the Father to remove the cup and free to respond in his own way. And yet, he trusts God the Father entirely: he addresses the Father both in the Aramaic "Abba" and the Greek πατήρ and concludes his prayer by subordinating his will to the Father. "Not what I want, but what you want."

How great is Jesus' persistence to pray this again and again! How great is Jesus' trust in the Father! He trusts that the Father hears his prayer. Much more, he expresses faith in the Father's will even facing the hour of his death. In this way, Jesus' will and the Father's will are persistent: to save humanity, the world, and you and me.

DEFINITION: CONTINUOUS PAST

***Continuous Past** indicates action in the past that is in progress, customary, or repeated, without reference to its completion. Most grammars call this the "Imperfect Tense." When you read Greek textbooks (and look at Bible software like BibleWorks or Accordance) you will need to think:

Continuous Past

*Imperfect Tense = Continuous Past

When parsing, remember to write "Continuous" as the aspect and "Past" as the time. In order to emphasize aspect in Greek, we are separating "tense" into aspect and time.

SIMILARITIES

1. The function of the Continuous Past in both Greek and English are similar. In general, this combination of aspect and time is used either to refer to an action in progress in the past, a customary action in the past, or a repeated or persistent action in the past.

a. Action in progress in past time

Jesus was teaching in their synagogues.

"Was teaching" indicates an action in progress in past time. There is no view of its completion, beginning or end. The emphasis is on the on-going nature of the action.

b. Customary action in past time

Most days Peter and Andrew were fishing, but now they follow Jesus.

In context, it is clear that "were fishing" refers to Peter and Andrew's customary action. We can emphasize this further in English by use of the words "used to":

Most days Peter and Andrew used to fish, but now they follow Jesus.

c. Repeated or persistent action in past time

The disciples were questioning Jesus about the parables.

In context, it may be clear that the Continuous Past refers to an action repeated many times, perhaps persistently. In this case, you may use "kept on" to communicate this nuance:

The disciples kept on questioning Jesus about the parables.

2. **Provide background for other action.** The Continuous Past may be used to contrast another verb in the simple (aorist) aspect. We will discuss this further in the next chapter but for now note how the Continuous Past provides background for other actions:

Jesus was teaching in the synagogue when a man with an unclean spirit came in.

The continuous past "was teaching" gives the background setting for the man to come in (in the aorist).

DIFFERENCES

1. English uses the past forms of "be" (was, were) and present participles to express the continuous past. English also will use other verbs, such as "used to" or "kept on" to clarify customary or repeated action.

2. Greek adds an epsilon before the stem to indicate the past time and uses secondary endings. So, to make the continuous past, take a continuous aspect stem, add an epsilon augment, and use *secondary* endings:

    Take the continuous stem   λύ-ω (I am loosing)
    And add an epsilon and secondary endings   ἐ + λύ + ον
    and Voila! You have the Cont. Act. Ind. Past   ἔλυον (I was loosing)

3. If the verb is deponent in present time, it will be deponent in past time too, using the middle/passive secondary endings:

    ἐπορεύετο => ἐ + πορεύ + ετο => C. Dep. Ind. Past. 3rd Sing. of πορεύ-ομαι
        (He/she/it) was journeying

4. The epsilon augment goes between any prefixes and the stem. It is essential to have prepositions memorized so that you can detect prefixes and correctly identify the stem:

    ἀπέστελλεν => ἀπο + ε + στέλλ + εν => C. A. Ind. Past 3rd Sg of ἀποστελλ-ω
        (He/she/it) was sending

Note that ἐκ will change to ἐξ when followed by an epsilon:

    ἐξεπορεύετο => ἐκ + ε + πορεύ + ετο => C. A. Ind. Past 3rd Sg of ἐκπορεύ-ομαι
        (He/she/it) was journeying out

5. If the first letter of the stem is a vowel, the epsilon augment also will combine with it, often lengthening it to eta or omega:

    ἀκού-ω (I am hearing) => ἐ + ἀκου + ον => ἤκουον (I was hearing)

    ὀφείλ-ω (I am indebted) => ἐ + ὀφειλ + ον => ὤφειλον (I was indebted)

Continuous Past

One exception to memorize is the Continuous Past of ἔχ-ω. The initial epsilon lengthens with the augment to epsilon iota:

ἔχ-ω (I am having) => ἐ + ἔχ + ον => εἶχον (I was having)

EXERCISES

Rewrite the following sentences, changing verbs in the *continuous present* to the *continuous past*.

1. Jesus is coming to Bethany.

2. There they are giving him a dinner.

3. Martha is serving and Lazarus is sitting at the table.

4. Mary is taking a pound of costly perfume and is anointing his feet.

5. Jesus' feet are wiped by her hair. *(What case would "hair" be in Greek?)*

Rewrite the following sentences, changing verbs from the *simple (aorist) past* to the *continuous past*. If you think the action was customary, try including "used to" in the translation. If you think the action was persistent, try including "kept on."

6. The house filled with the fragrance of the perfume.

7. But Judas Iscariot complained.

8. He said this not because he cared about the poor, but because he stole from the common purse.

9. Jesus said, "She bought it for the day of my burial."

10. So the chief priests planned to put Lazarus to death as well.

12

Future Time

DEVOTION

And night will be no longer! and they will no longer need light from a lamp or light of the sun, because the LORD God will shine on them! and they will rule into the ages of ages! (Rev 22:5)

καὶ νὺξ οὐκ ἔσται ἔτι καὶ οὐκ ἔχουσιν χρείαν φωτὸς λύχνου καὶ φωτὸς ἡλίου, ὅτι κύριος ὁ θεὸς φωτίσει ἐπ' αὐτούς, καὶ βασιλεύσουσιν εἰς τοὺς αἰῶνας τῶν αἰώνων.

The book of Revelation comes to a close with this magnificent prediction of the future. In the New Jerusalem—the symbol of the future life with God and God's creation—there will be no need for light. Literally, light is necessary to see and so a lamp and the sun enable sight during the night and day. Therefore, figuratively, they compete with God for the role of illuminator. Because of the sun and lamps, we think we can see without God.

More specific to the book of Revelation, light enables work. Light from a lamp alludes to the lamps that are required for working inside buildings in the city and at night (see Rev 18:22–23). The light of the sun is necessary for agriculture and work outside, but also scorches laborers with its heat (see Rev 7:16; cf. 16:8–9). These lights shine on and direct our work. In the New Jerusalem, however, God is the one who will illuminate, enable, and direct our work.

Christian faith takes its cues not so much from what is but from what will be. For us, the future determines our relationships in the present. Since our life and work is illuminated and directed by God in the future, we live today free of other sources of "light" that may claim to guide our work. God alone is and will be our light!

DEFINITION: FUTURE TIME

***Future time** indicates action that has not yet taken place at the time of speaking. For example, "Jesus will come again to judge the living and the dead" describes a future event relative to the time of speaking.

FUTURE TIME

SIMILARITIES

In terms of function, Greek and English are almost equivalent when it comes to *future time. Both English and Greek use the future time to indicate an action that has not taken place yet. In both languages, the future also may be used for commands (e.g., "You will clean your room!") or in conditional sentences ("If you clean your room, I will thank you").

DIFFERENCES

1. English uses the auxiliary words "will" and "shall" before the verb to indicate future time. There are some rules for when to use "will" or "shall" but these are not often followed in English. In general, use "will" for the future and reserve "shall" for formal language or commands.

2. It should be no surprise by now: Greek changes the form of the verb to reflect future time. In Greek, a sigma is added after the stem and before personal endings. For example,

Take the continuous stem	λύ-ω (I am loosing)
And add a sigma before the personal endings	λύ + σ + ω
and Voila! You have the continuous-act-ind-future	λύσ-ω (I will loose)

This form is sometimes called the "Second Principal Part." Especially if you think you've spotted an irregular future form, you will want to remember that the continuous-future is *second*. It will appear in the second column of a list of principal parts.[1] For example, the future of the *deponent verb ἔρχ-ομαι is ἐλεύσ-ομαι. There's no way to predict this kind of radical future form! I suggest you make a separate flash card for the future forms that don't follow the usual rules.

3. Sigma combines with some consonants (especially p- and k-sounds), so look for the future's sigma in psi and xi.[2]

βλέπ-ω (I am looking at) => βλέπ + σ + ω => βλέψ-ω (I will be looking at)

4. With contract verbs (ά-ω, έ-ω, ό-ω), the contract vowel will be lengthened before the sigma to eta in alpha and epsilon contract verbs, and omega for omicron contract verbs:

ἀγαπά-ω (I am loving) => ἀγαπά + σ + ω => ἀγαπήσ-ω (I will be loving)

---

1. Check the back of your Greek textbook for a list of principle parts. Croy does not have a list; there is a master list in the back of Mounce, *BBG*, 370–80.
2. See the "square of stops" in Croy, *Primer*, 66, and Mounce, *BBG*, 161.

ποιέ-ω (I am doing) => ποιέ + σ + ω => ποιήσ-ω (I will be doing)

πληρό-ω (I am filling) => πληρό + σ + ω => πληρώσ-ω (I will be filling)

5. When the verb is not conjugated, I am emphasizing using a dash between the stem and the personal endings. This is (1) to help you find the words in the lexicon (contract verbs always are listed with the uncontracted vowel). (2) It is also to help you see clearly where the sigma goes and how it may affect the stem.

6. English and Greek have different expressions of Aspect with Future Time. In English, there is a form of each aspect in Future Time:

Continuous:	I will be doing
Simple (Aorist):	I will do
Perfect:	I will have done

In Greek there is no Aorist Active Indicative Future, so in many cases the Continuous Active Indicative Future will have a simple meaning. Your default translation should still be continuous, but be ready to switch to a simple aspect if it makes more sense in context.

βλέψομεν τὴν δόξαν αὐτοῦ.
We will be looking at his glory.
or
We will look at his glory.

Is the context emphasizing the continuous examination of his glory in the future? Or a simple event? Only context will tell. (Note that the issue is significant to interpretation!)

7. Celebrate! The personal endings for future time in the active and middle voice are the primary endings you have already learned. In general, verbs that are *deponent in the present are also *deponent in the future. Some verbs that are active in present time are *deponent in the future, which means that in the future they are middle in form but active in meaning. The most important of these is εἰμί. The bad news: The future passive is a different animal that we will meet later.

EXERCISES

For the following exercises, pay special attention to how the auxiliary verbs ("be," "do," etc.) change in English depending on the time of the verb.

Rewrite the following sentences, changing the verbs in *past time into future time*.
   1. Jesus looked at the rich man, and loved him.

Future Time

2. Teacher, I have kept all the commandments.

3. You lacked one thing.

4. When he heard this, he was shocked.

5. And he went away grieving because he had many possessions.

Rewrite the following sentences, changing verbs from the future time to present time. **Emphasize a continuous aspect when you write the verb in present time.**

6. You shall not murder.

7. You will give him the name Jesus, because he will save his people from their sins.

8. Not one stone will be left on another, for all will be thrown down.

9. How hard it will be for those who have wealth to enter the kingdom of God!

10. Then, who will be saved?

13

Aorist Aspect

DEVOTION

But God is demonstrating his own love for us, in that while we were still sinners Christ died for us. (Romans 5:8)

συνίστησιν δὲ τὴν ἑαυτοῦ ἀγάπην εἰς ἡμᾶς ὁ θεός, ὅτι ἔτι ἁμαρτωλῶν ὄντων ἡμῶν Χριστὸς ὑπὲρ ἡμῶν ἀπέθανεν.

Aspect plays a huge role in this verse. There are three verbal forms: (1) God *is demonstrating*. "Is demonstrating" is continuous present. As Paul writes, God is in the process of demonstrating love for us. On one level, God's love is continuously demonstrated whenever it is announced that Christ died for us. On another, Paul's very words are demonstrating this fact. (2) We *were* sinners. The continuous aspect here emphasizes that the state of Sin was ongoing and continuous. Like the aspect of the verb, we were inside the action, inside the state of Sin and unable to get outside of it. This continuous state of sin is the background for the main action: (3) Christ *died* (ἀπέθανεν) for us. The Aorist aspect of this verb (the lexical form is ἀποθνῄσκ-ω) in context is punctiliar, a point in time interrupting the continuous state of sin we were in.

God is demonstrating love, even now, when it is proclaimed that "while we were still sinners, Christ died for us."

DEFINITION: AORIST ASPECT

The *Aorist Aspect indicates "simple" or "undefined" action. In Greek, the word "aorist" means "undefined." This aspect is undefined in the sense that its viewpoint must be determined in context. However, we can say that the aorist aspect views the action from the outside, and can focus on various parts of the action or the action as a whole. It can view the beginning of the action, its end, or the whole action.

AORIST ASPECT

SIMILARITIES

1. English also has a simple aspect:

Jesus walked by the sea

The action gives no indication about its continuity or completion—it is undefined. The context may supply these details, but the verb itself does not suggest them.

2. English and Greek will both may use the continuous aspect to provide background for action in the simple aspect:

While Peter and Andrew were fishing in their boats, Jesus walked by the sea.

The continuous "were fishing" provides background for the foreground action: Jesus walked by. The aspects of the verbs are like stage directions for a movie: the camera is showing Peter and Andrew fishing. There is no sense when they began fishing or when they will end. Suddenly the camera pulls back to show Jesus walking by on the beach with Peter and Andrew fishing in the background. The focus is on the simple verb.

3. Both English and Greek have "regular" (more obvious) ways to form the aorist (simple) past. In English, the regular way is to add "-ed" to the end of the verb. "Irregular" English forms are harder to predict, as they often are in Greek.

walk + ed => walked

Jesus walked

but *Peter and Andrew* swam *across the sea.*

DIFFERENCES

1. Greek uses the **aorist aspect stem** to form aorist verbs.

To make a **"regular" (1st) aorist stem** you will add a sigma alpha to the continuous stem:

Begin with the continuous stem	λύ-ω (I am loosing)
Add a sigma alpha	λύ + σα-
and voila! You have the aorist stem	λύσα-

Also, note that when you add sigma alpha, the sigma will cause any contract vowels to lengthen, and will combine with consonantal stops (π, β, φ, κ, γ, χ, τ, δ, θ). This is identical to the way the sigma of future time combines with stems. E.g., the 1st aorist stem of βλέπ-ω:

$$\beta\lambda\acute{\epsilon}\pi\text{-}\omega \text{ (I am looking at)} \Rightarrow \beta\lambda\acute{\epsilon}\pi + \sigma\alpha\text{-} \Rightarrow \beta\lambda\epsilon\psi\alpha\text{-}$$

Note: This is only the aorist stem! It is not yet conjugated, but you need to know this so you can make participles, infinitives, etc. out of the stem.

You may look at the sigma and fear confusing it with the sigma that marks future time. A key difference will be the alpha. We will work at some strategies to avoid this confusion.

2. Some Greek verbs have an **"irregular" (2nd) Aorist stem**. There are no easy rules to learn to make these stems—they have to be memorized. (I suggest a separate card for the Aorist stem, as well as perhaps a master card with all of the stems on it).

For example, some of the most important forms are:

Lexical Form		Continuous Stem	Aorist Stem
ἔρχ-ομαι	I am coming/going	ἐρχ-	ἐλθ-
γίν-ομαι	I am becoming	γιν-	γεν-
λαμβάν-ω	I am taking, receiving	λαμβαν-	λαβ-
ἀποθνῄσκ-ω	I am dying	ἀπο-θνῃσκ-	ἀπο-θαν-
βάλλ-ω	I am throwing	βαλλ-	βαλ-

In general, 2nd aorist stems will look like a shorter form of the continuous stem

When memorizing stems, I encourage you to leave the dashes after the stem to remind you that it is a stem and not yet a conjugated form. A dash between prepositional prefixes and the stem will also help you remember where the augment goes.

3. **When in the indicative mood, the aorist aspect is almost always in past time.**[1] conjugating the aorist indicative in past time follows a similar procedure as we saw with the continuous aspect.

4. **For past time:** Greek adds an epsilon before the stem to indicate the past time and uses secondary endings. So, to make the aorist past, take an aorist aspect stem, add an epsilon augment, and use secondary endings (See for example, Croy p. 78; Mounce p. 196). This procedure works perfectly for 2nd aorist verbs. For example, to make the aorist past of λαμβάν-ω (I am receiving):

Take the aorist stem	λαβ-
And add an epsilon and secondary endings	ἐ + λαβ + ον
and Voila! You have the Aorist Act. Ind. Past	ἔλαβον (I received)

---

1. The only exception to this is the Aorist Passive Indicative Future (Croy lesson 16 and Mounce chapter 24). In Greek there are no Aorist Indicative Present forms.

Aorist Aspect

Conjugating the 1st aorist is different because of the alpha that ends the 1st aorist stem. Essentially, the alpha becomes the connecting vowel (except in the 3rd singular). The 1st singular does not use the usual nu ending. (See the tables in your Greek textbook, e.g., Croy p. 72 and Mounce p. 205.) For example, to make the aorist past of λύ-ω (I am loosing):

Take the aorist stem	λυσα-
And add an epsilon and secondary endings	ἐ + λυσα + -
and Voila! You have the Aorist Act. Ind. Past	ἔλυσα (I loosed)

RECOGNITION

1. To recognize the aorist, follow the same procedure that we began with the continuous past:

   a. Identify and isolate the ending: Is it a personal ending? If so, what person and number?
   b. Identify and isolate any prefixes: Is there an augment? If so, then it is past time.
   c. Identify the stem: Is it continuous or aorist (the two aspects we have covered)?

   ἐλάβομεν => ἐ + λαβ + ομεν => Aorist Act. Ind. Past. 1st Pl. of λαμβάν-ω
   We received

2. **If the first letter of the stem is a vowel, the epsilon augment will combine with it**, often lengthening it to eta or omega. (See Croy p. 54 or Mounce pp. 185–6 for more examples.)

   ἔρχ-ομαι (*I am coming/going*) => ε + ἐλθ + ον => ἦλθον (*I came/went*)

Note that ἔρχ-ομαι is deponent in the continuous stem (i.e., uses middle/passive endings but is active in meaning) but in the aorist stem is active in form and meaning.

3. **Remember that the epsilon augment goes between any prefixes and the stem.**

   ἐξῆλθεν => ἐκ + ε + ελθ + εν => Aorist A. Ind. Past 3rd Sg of ἐξέρχ-ομαι
   (He/she/it) went out.

Note that ἐκ will change to ἐξ when followed by a vowel.

4. **Avoiding Confusion with the Future.** To avoid confusion with the future, first think of the -σα- as a part of the aorist stem *not* a time formative (the sigma used with future time). We will see the -σα- of the 1st Aorist in other moods independent of time.

Second, when you see the sigma ask yourself:
(1) Is there an augment? It is a sure sign of past time and rules out the future.
(2) Are there secondary endings? It again will rule out the future.

5. **Confusion between 1st singular and 3rd plural endings.** We noticed with the secondary endings that the 1st singular and 3rd plural endings are both -ον. So, for 2nd aorist verbs only context will tell you which person it is:

$$\text{ἔλαβον} = I\ received\ \text{or}\ They\ received.$$

In context:

$$\text{ἐγὼ ἔλαβον τὴν σοφίαν.}$$
$$I\ received\ wisdom.$$

$$\text{αὐτοὶ ἔλαβον τὴν σοφίαν.}$$
$$They\ received\ wisdom.$$

This is not a problem for the 1st aorist. The key is the final nu:

$$\text{ἔλυσα} = I\ loosed \quad \text{and} \quad \text{ἔλυσαν} = They\ loosed$$

EXERCISES

Rewrite the following sentences, changing verbs in the *continuous past* to the *aorist past*.

1. Jesus was coming to Galilee.

2. He was testifying the word of God.

3. The Galileans were welcoming him.

4. They were seeing everything he was doing at the festival.

5. They also were going to the festival.

Rewrite the following sentences, changing verbs from the *aorist past* to the *continuous past*. If you think the action could be customary, try including "used to" in the translation. If you think the action could be persistent, try including "kept on."

Aorist Aspect

6. Then he came to Cana in Galilee.

7. A royal official heard that Jesus came to Galilee.

8. He begged him to heal his son.

9. Jesus said to him, "Will you believe if you see signs?"

10. The man believed the word that Jesus spoke to him.

14

Perfect Aspect

DEVOTION

Now they have known that everything, as much as you have given me, is from you. (John 17:7)

νῦν ἔγνωκαν ὅτι πάντα ὅσα δέδωκάς μοι παρὰ σοῦ εἰσιν·

In his "Farewell Discourse" to the disciples, Jesus uses two perfect present verbs to express completed events that have significant effects for the present moment. The first, ἔγνωκαν, which I have translated "they have known," emphasizes that the disciples have come to a state of knowledge about Jesus: they know that he is from the Father and that his words are from the Father. In this context, the perfect expresses the completion of their appropriation of that knowledge and that they remain in this state. One way to emphasize this may be to translate it "they have come to know."

The second perfect, δέδωκάς, "you have given," emphasizes that the action of the Father's giving of knowledge to Jesus is complete—as much as was given to Jesus—and has the abiding effect of knowledge for the disciples. This is the theme of this part of John 17: that the chain of revelation is complete. The disciples know that the Father gave "the words" (τὰ ῥήματα in v. 8) to the Son, and the Son has given these words to the disciples. These acts of revelation are complete, but have abiding effects into the moment of speaking. For John, this abiding knowledge of God the Father through Jesus is extended to the audience and to us. We have come to know God through Jesus.

DEFINITION: PERFECT ASPECT

The ***Perfect Aspect** indicates that an action has been brought to its appropriate completion in a way that its effects remain.

PERFECT ASPECT

SIMILARITIES

1. Both English and Greek use the perfect to describe some action that has been completed and has lasting effects. For example:

You have filled Jerusalem with your teaching. (Acts 5:28)
πεπληρώκατε τὴν Ἰερουσαλὴμ τῆς διδαχῆς ὑμῶν.

In both English and Greek, the subject ("you," pl.) has completed the action ("filled"). At the time of speaking, the fact that the apostles are filling Jerusalem with their teaching remains—and is a problem for the High Priest who is speaking here in Acts.

2. For the perfect indicative, both English and Greek use the time of a perfect verb to indicate the point in time that the effects of the completed action are felt.

a. Perfect Present. If the effect of the action is experienced at the time of speaking, then the perfect present is used (as in the example above). We can draw this as a dot with an extending line and an arrow to mark the point of interest. The time of the verb and the moment of speaking are identical (i.e., present):

☺ = moment of speaking

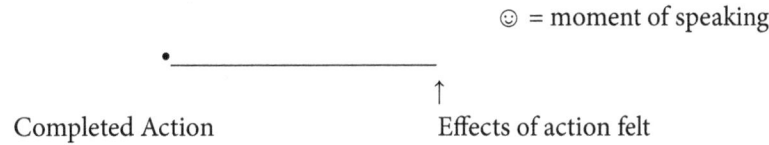

Completed Action   Effects of action felt

Note that the perfect does *not* inherently indicate that the effects are permanent or extend beyond that point. In context, such a meaning may be inferred, but it is too much to assume from the grammar alone.

b. Perfect Past. When the effect of the completed action is felt in the Past of the speaker, then the Perfect Past is used. This can be visualized:

☺ = moment of speaking

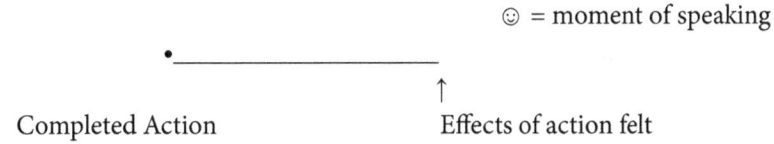

Completed Action   Effects of action felt

Again, note that the perfect does not indicate that the effects continue past the point of evaluation, even at the time of speaking.

For example, consider the story of the house built on the rock. It did not fall when the rains and flood and winds came because

It had been founded on the rock. (Matt 7:25)
τεθεμελίωτο γὰρ ἐπὶ τὴν πέτραν.

As Jesus tells this story, he refers to a point in the past when rains and flood came. But the focus of the perfect "had been founded" is that before the rains and flood came, the house had been founded on rock. The founding was a completed action that had lasting effects: a strong house that could withstand rains, flood and wind.

The perfect past is often called the *pluperfect tense in other grammars. Be sure to remember

Perfect Past = *Pluperfect

DIFFERENCES

1. The English perfect present uses present forms of "have" with past participles. For example:

You have filled Jerusalem.

I have fought the good fight.

The English perfect past uses past forms of "have" (e.g., "had") with past participles. For example:

It had been founded on rock.

Paul had told the Galatians the truth about Jesus Christ, and they believed.

2. The English perfect has a broader meaning than the Greek perfect, overlapping with the Greek Aorist. The English perfect can refer to events that happened in some indefinite time in the past as well as events that just happened.

The following table may make this clearer:[1]

The **English Simple Past** expresses an action that took place at a definite time in the past, or an action between then and the time of speaking, of which the speaker wishes to suggest an interval.	The **Greek Aorist** expresses an action simply as an event without any indication of its progress or result.
For example: *Jesus walked near the sea.* This suggests that at some specific time in the past Jesus walked near the sea.	

---

1. Adapted from Nunn, *Short Syntax*, 75.

Perfect Aspect

The **English Perfect** expresses an action that took place at an indefinite past time, or an action between then and the time of speaking that the speaker does not wish to suggest an interval. **For example:** *Jesus has walked near the sea.* This does not suggest any definite time, only the fact that at some point Jesus has walked near the sea.	**For example:** ὁ Ἰησοῦς ἐπορεύθη παρὰ τὴν θάλασσαν. (*Jesus traveled near the sea.*) This may refer to a definite or indefinite event. Context rules!
The **English Perfect** expresses an action regarded as complete at the time of speaking whose results are regarded as still existing. **For example:** *Jesus has walked near the sea and his footprints are still there.* This focuses on the results at the time of speaking.	The **Greek Perfect** expresses an action regarded as complete at the time of speaking whose results are regarded as still existing. For example: ὁ Ἰησοῦς πεπόρευται παρὰ τὴν θάλασσαν καὶ ἔτι ἴχνος αὐτοῦ ἐστιν. (*Jesus traveled near the sea and still his footprint is there.*) In this Greek sentence, the Perfect focuses on the result of the completed action.

3. In Greek, the perfect aspect active voice is indicated by a change in stem. To make regular perfect active stems, for example, with λύ-ω:

Take the continuous stem	λύ-
Reduplicate the first letter followed by an epsilon	λ + ε + λύ- = λελυ-
Add kappa alpha to the end	λελυ + κα = λέλυκα-
Voila! You have your perfect active stem, ready to conjugate	**λέλυκα-**
e.g., "We have loosed"	λελύκαμεν

For perfect middle or passive stems, omit the kappa alpha:

Take the continuous stem	λύ-
Reduplicate the first letter followed by an epsilon	λ + ε + λύ- = λελυ-
Voila! You have your perfect mid/pass stem, ready to conjugate	**λέλυ-**
e.g., "We have been loosed"	λελύμεθα

4. Predictably, Greek **Perfect Indicative Present** uses primary endings, but note a connecting vowel is not used (see Croy p. 84 or Mounce p. 225).

The **Perfect Active Indicative Present is the fourth column of principle parts** (see Croy §105, p. 87; Mounce p. 226). Charts of principal parts can be very useful for recognizing verbal forms, but if you know how stems change and your verbal endings, you can figure it out.

ἐκβάλλ-ω => ἐκ + βέβληκα => ἐκβέβληκα

The **Perfect Middle/Passive Indicative Present is the fifth column of the principle parts.**

$$\text{ἐκβάλλ-ω} => \text{ἐκ} + \text{βέβλη} + \text{μαι} => \text{ἐκβέβλημαι}$$

5. The Greek **Perfect Indicative Past** (aka **Pluperfect**) is rare in the NT, only occurring 53 times (not counting the past of οἶδα, which is really a perfect form). Predictably, you make the past time by adding an epsilon augment in front of the stem and using secondary endings.

Note that the alpha ending of the stem changes to ει for the Perfect Past:

$$\text{ἐ} + \text{λελύκει} + \text{ν}$$

ἐλελύκειν
I had loosed

See Croy §104, p. 86 or Mounce pp. 234–5. Note that sometimes the augment is not included.

RECOGNIZING THE PERFECT

We have two points that help us recognize the Perfect Aspect:

1. Reduplication of the first consonant. Recognizing reduplication is complicated by the following:

a. If the first letter of the continuous stem is an aspirated consonant (φ, χ, or θ), the unaspirated consonant (π, κ, or τ) is reduplicated (see Croy §103, pp. 85–6 or Mounce p. 226). For example:

φανερό-ω => πεφανέρωκα
I reveal => I have revealed

b. If the first letter of the continuous stem is a vowel or diphthong, it is lengthened.

ἀγαπά-ω => ἠγάπηκα
I love => I have loved

In these cases, the key to recognition is the -κα in the active voice.

c. If the verb has one or more prepositional prefixes, the reduplication occurs after the prefixes. This is no surprise, as we've seen how inflection (like the past time augment) affects the stem not prefixes.

2. The -κα- for the Perfect Active. For example, λελύκαμεν ("We have loosed").

PERFECT ASPECT

EXERCISES

Rewrite the following sentences, changing verbs in the *aorist past* to the *perfect present*.

1. I wrote about all that Jesus did and taught.

2. Jesus was taken up into heaven.

3. He gave instructions through the Holy Spirit to the apostles whom he chose.

4. After he suffered, he presented himself alive to them.

5. He appeared to them for forty days and spoke about the royal rule of God.

Rewrite the following sentences, changing the verbs from the *perfect present* to the *aorist past*.

6. While he has stayed with them, he has ordered them not to leave Jerusalem.

7. Instead, they have waited there for the promise of the Father.

8. He has said, "This is what you have heard from me.

9. John has baptized with water, but you will be baptized with the Holy Spirit.

10. When they have come together, they have asked him many questions.

15

Participles

DEVOTION

To the one who is loving us and who loosed us from our sins by his blood, . . . (Rev 1:5)

Τῷ ἀγαπῶντι ἡμᾶς καὶ λύσαντι ἡμᾶς ἐκ τῶν ἁμαρτιῶν ἡμῶν ἐν τῷ αἵματι αὐτοῦ, . . .

Participles are verbal adjectives. As such they retain the action of a verb and acquire the descriptive power of adjectives. In this example, John describes Jesus using two participles, ἀγαπῶντι and λύσαντι. The first is the continuous aspect and describes Jesus as the one who continually loves believers. The second is the aorist aspect and describes Jesus as the one who acted to loose us, to free us from our sins, by his blood. Both participles emphasize Jesus' action as one who loves and one who frees. Together they describe Jesus' continuous love shown most poignantly in his death on the cross, where he shed his blood as the Lamb of God.

DEFINITION: PARTICIPLE

A *Participle is a verbal adjective. This means that it has *aspect and *voice like every verb, but has *case, *gender and *number like adjectives. Just as adjectives can be used as nouns, participles also can be used as nouns (in English called gerunds).

SIMILARITIES

There are four basic uses of a participle in both English and Greek.

1. *Substantive. The participle is used in place of a noun, sometimes with an article:

We anticipate the <u>coming</u> of the Lord.

Participles

"Coming" is a participle in English (note the ending "-ing"). The article "the" communicates that it is functioning as a noun, a definite "coming." Just as adjectives can be made to function as nouns, so participles (verbal adjectives) can function like a noun.

Note that "the coming" is functioning as the direct object of the verb "anticipate." In Greek, the participle would have the case that reflects its function in the sentence. *What case and number would "the coming" be in Greek?*

For substantive participles in Greek, you will add the phrase "the one" in place of the definite article (or "the thing" for neuter):

ὁ πιστεύων εἰς αὐτόν . . .
The one believing in him . . .

It also may make sense in context to use "the one who . . ." (or "the thing that . . ." for neuters) followed by a finite form of the verb. If you do this, be sure to maintain the aspect and voice of the participle.

ὁ πιστεύων εἰς αὐτόν . . .
The one who is believing in him . . .

2. *Periphrastic.* "Peri" (around) + "phrasis" (speaking) simply means "a round about way of speaking," or using more words than necessary to say something. In this case, some form of "be" may be used with a participle to communicate the same thing as a single verb.

In English, we use periphrasis for the continuous aspect:

Jesus *is coming*.

The verb "is" plus the participle "coming" indicates that the action is in process.

The participle can be used the same way in Greek:

ὁ Ἰησοῦς ἐστὶν ἐρχόμενος.
Jesus is *coming*.

In Greek, the meaning is the same as

ὁ Ἰησοῦς ἔρχεται.
Jesus is coming.

which is why we call it "periphrastic" to use a form of "be" (εἰμί or γίνομαι) and a participle. It is a "round about" way of speaking.

3. Attributive. In both Greek and English, participles are used to modify nouns and pronouns. For example:

Brushing Up English to Learn Greek

The disciple <u>sitting at Jesus' right hand</u> leaned on him.

The phrase "sitting at Jesus' right hand" modifies the noun "disciple," answering the question "Which disciple?" In Greek the participle will appear generally in attributive position with the noun it modifies and match it in **case, gender, number, and definiteness** (recall this from our discussion of adjectives).[1]

4. Adverbial. These participles do not modify nouns, but act like adverbs: they modify verbs, other adverbs or adjectives (most often verbs).

<u>Looking at the ground</u>, the centurion approached Jesus.

"Looking at the ground" describes *how* the centurion approached; therefore it modifies the verb "approached." It does not communicate which centurion (which would make it attributive).

In English we sometimes clarify the participle's precise function by translating it with an adverbial clause. Eight kinds of adverbial clauses are listed below. *Which ones do you think are appropriate for the above sentence?* Some of these do not seem to fit in context.

	Answers for main verb:	
Temporal	When?	**When** looking at the ground . . .
Causal	Why?	**Because** he is looking at the ground, . . .
Manner	In what manner?	**By** looking at the ground, . . .
Means	By what means?	**By means of** looking at the ground . . .
Concessive	What hinders?	**Although** looking at the ground, . . .
Conditional	Under what condition?	**If** looking at the ground, . . .
Purpose	For what purpose?	**In order to** look at the ground, . . .
Circumstantial	In what circumstance?	simply "-ing" or "**While** . . ."

If the participle is adverbial in Greek, you will have to decide between these options based on context. In general, you should start with the default "-ing" but think about its specific meaning in context. Memorize the above list so that you know what is available. Adverbial participles are one of the most exciting parts about translating Greek—you can explore some very different options (for example, compare the temporal with the concessive in the sentence above).

5. Participial Phrases. Because participles are verb forms, they can have direct objects and indirect objects and be modified by adverbs and prepositional phrases. When you see a participle, look for these things and bracket the participial phrase in order to avoid

---

1. Participles can also be predicative, but this is relatively rare.

confusion. Note how the sentence still makes sense even when you remove the participial phrase. Take the following examples:

The one [sitting on the throne] is like an emerald in appearance.

- The participle "sitting" is modified by the prepositional phrase "on the throne."
- It is a substantive participle, and the whole phrase "the one sitting on the throne" functions as the subject of the main verb "is." *What case would you expect "sitting" to be in Greek?*
- In Greek, it would appear as the definite article + participle of "sitting" + prepositional phrase "on the throne." (The translator supplies "the one.")

[Giving thanks to God for their many blessings], the disciples shared bread and wine.

- The participle "giving" has a direct object "thanks," an indirect object "to God" and a prepositional phrase "for their many blessings."
- The whole participial phrase is adverbial, modifying the main verb "shared."

DIFFERENCES

1. English generally adds "-ing" to make the active participle and "-ed" to make the passive participle.

2. Greek uses one of the aspect stems (continuous, aorist, or perfect) and adds a morpheme followed by the case endings we've learned. You can find the details in your Greek textbook. Don't worry about it right now. Our job is to focus on how participles function in similar ways in Greek and English.

EXERCISES

Circle each participle in the following sentences and identify each as either substantive, periphrastic, attributive, **or adverbial.**

1. God will judge the living and the dead.

2. The running father threw his arms around his son.

3. His son begged for forgiveness, weeping and wailing.

4. The woman is drawing water from the deep well.

5. Jesus offers her living water.

Circle each participle and draw brackets around the participial phrase, including any objects or prepositional phrases that link to the participle.

6. Every eye will see the one coming on the clouds.

7. The tax collector confessed his sin, hanging his head in shame.

8. The one believing in him will have eternal life.

9. Kneeling before Jesus, the rich man asked, "What must I do?"

10. Jesus said, "Everyone hearing my word and doing it is like a wise man building his house on rock."

16

Subjunctive—the Mood of Possibility

DEVOTION

"The thief does not come except in order to steal and kill and destroy; I came in order that they may have life and have it abundantly." (John 10:10)

ὁ κλέπτης οὐκ ἔρχεται εἰ μὴ ἵνα κλέψῃ καὶ θύσῃ καὶ ἀπολέσῃ· ἐγὼ ἦλθον ἵνα ζωὴν ἔχωσιν καὶ περισσὸν ἔχωσιν.

What is our purpose? What is God's purpose? These are big questions that human beings ask when they have time to contemplate meaning or when life has gone so horribly wrong that fundamental assumptions must be questioned. Purpose is at the heart of these questions.

There are many ways to express purpose in Greek. One of the most common uses for the subjunctive mood in the Greek NT is following the conjunction ἵνα, "in order that." This word introduces a purpose clause; it explains the purpose of the main verb. In the above sentence, it explains why the thief comes and why Jesus comes. The thief comes to steal, kill, and destroy. Jesus comes that "the sheep" (i.e., those who believe in him and hear his voice) may have life and have it abundantly.

When we start to question our purpose and God's purpose in the world, it's a good idea to start looking at ἵνα clauses. Jesus comes in order that we might have abundant life. Jesus lays down his life in order to take it up again (John 10:17). God gave his only Son in order that everyone who believes in him may not perish but have eternal life (John 3:16).

DEFINITION: SUBJUNCTIVE MOOD

The ***Subjunctive** mood expresses possibility or condition that is distinguished from reality. In general, we use auxiliaries such as "may" or "might" with the verb for the subjunctive in English. This is somewhat an unreliable way to translate the Greek subjunctive, so be ready to discard "may" or "might" in your translation.[1] The subjunctive is especially important in some conditional statements ("if . . . then").

SIMILARITIES

The subjunctive is used in both English and Greek for exhortations, deliberation, and conditions, but its use (and forms) in English are fading.

1. Hortatory Subjunctive. The speaker exhorts others to act. "Let . . ." is a helpful way to translate these subjunctives. The action is not reality; the speaker uses the subjunctive to exhort that the possibility may become reality. (The Beatles sang, "Let it be, let it be . . .")

<u>Let us go across</u> to the other side. (Mark 4:35)
διέλθωμεν εἰς τὸ πέραν.

2. Deliberative Subjunctive. When a speaker is asking a question about a course of action and the outcome is uncertain, the subjunctive mood expresses that the action is not reality but possibility. In English, we may use the auxiliaries "should" or "shall" in front of these questions.

<u>Should we continue</u> in sin in order that grace may abound? (Rom 6:1)
ἐπιμένωμεν τῇ ἁμαρτίᾳ, ἵνα ἡ χάρις πλεονάσῃ;

Paul is asking a question to deliberate and uses the subjunctive mood to express that continuing in sin is possible. In this case, the answer is obvious ("No way!" he says in Rom 6:2) but in other cases the answer is truly uncertain.

3. Conditions. A conditional statement is an "if . . .then" statement. The "if" clause is called the *protasis, the clause expressing the condition (think πρό = "in front of"). The "then" clause is called the *apodosis, the clause expressing the consequence (think ἀπό = "away from" the condition). In Greek, the subjunctive follows the particle ἐάν in the protasis.

<u>If we confess</u> our sins, he is faithful and just. . . (1 John 1:9)
ἐὰν ὁμολογῶμεν τὰς ἁμαρτίας ἡμῶν, πιστός ἐστιν καὶ δίκαιος. . .

Note that we did not use "may" in the final translation. You may have started out writing "If we may confess our sins. . ." but recognized that it didn't work in English.

---

1. In general the rule is to use "may" when the main verb is in present time, "might" when the main verb is in past time. Remember that the subjunctive verb will not have time!

Subjunctive—the Mood of Possibility

The meaning of the conditional sentence is important to recognize: If the protasis is true (we confess our sins), the "then" clause is true (God is faithful and just). The use of ἐάν + subjunctive in the *protasis and the present indicative in the *apodosis is called a **present general condition** and is common in the Greek NT. It expresses a condition that functions as general rule in the present.

Another kind of conditional is called a **future more vivid condition**. This also uses ἐάν + subjunctive in the protasis, but the future indicative in the apodosis. This expresses an assumption about the future and its likely consequence. For example, "*If it is* (ἐὰν ᾖ) *advisable for me to go, they will go* (πορεύσονται) *with me*" (1 Cor 16:4).

There are other kinds of conditional statements that do not use the subjunctive in the protasis; don't worry about them now.

DIFFERENCES

1. Forms. English uses "be" for all forms in the present subjunctive and "were" for all forms in the past subjunctive.

If he be here, I will help him.
If they were here, they would not be there.

In Greek, the subjunctive form is constructed by taking an aspect stem and lengthening the connecting vowel. **This lengthened connecting vowel is a key way to recognize the subjunctive.** An omicron connecting vowel is lengthened to omega and an epsilon is lengthened to an eta (iotas in endings then become subscripted under the eta). For example, with λύ-ω:

Take the Continuous Stem	λύ-
Add an ending (here 2nd person singular)	λυ + ε + ις[2]
Lengthen the connecting vowel	λυ + η + ις
Subscript the iota under the eta	λυ + ῃ + ς
Voila! You have the 2nd person Continuous Subjunctive	**λύῃς**

See Croy pp. 137–8 or Mounce pp. 290–1 for a list of forms. Note that the Cont. Act. **Subj.** 1st Sing. is λύω, identical in form to the Cont. Act. **Ind.** Present 1st Sing. The only way to tell the difference is context!

The aorist subjunctive will not have an augment, since the augment is a sign of time not aspect. This will be your main help to distinguish the aorist indicative from the aorist subjunctive.

λύσω (first aorist active subjunctive of λύ-ω)[3] I may loose

---

[2]. The 2nd person singular primary ending originally was -σι, but became reversed (see Smyth §463b).

[3]. Note this is also the form for the indicative future! Context will help you tell the difference; look for ἵνα and ἄν and other indications of the subjunctive.

ἔλθῃ   (second aorist active subjunctive of ἔρχ-ομαι)[4]   He/she/it may come/go

2. Greek uses one of the **aspect stems (continuous, aorist, or perfect)**. Recall that only Indicative verbs have time; the Subjunctive does not express time. The aspect of the verb is very important! Try to preserve the sense in your translations. The **continuous aspect** in Greek may be emphasized in English by using "continue to . . ." with an infinitive of the verb. For example: λύῃς may be translated "you may continue to loose." See what works best in context.

3. **Look for the subjunctive following ἵνα** ("in order that"). ἵνα introduces a **purpose** clause. I strongly suggest *always* translating ἵνα as "in order that," especially to distinguish it from a **result** clause introduced by ὥστε ("so that," usually followed by an infinitive).

Should we continue in sin <u>in order that</u> grace may abound? (Rom 6:1)
ἐπιμένωμεν τῇ ἁμαρτίᾳ, ἵνα ἡ χάρις πλεονάσῃ;

4. **Look for the subjunctive following words with ἄν.** The particle ἄν (untranslatable by itself) suggests that a verb is modified by some condition. It is often combined by elision with other words:

εἰ ("if") + ἄν   = ἐάν (also translated "if")
ὅτε ("when") + ἄν   = ὅταν ("whenever")
καί ("and") + ἐάν ("if") = κἄν ("and if")
(note how the breathing mark remains as a hint of elision)

Sometimes you'll see an ἄν after a relative pronoun. In this situation, translate them as "whoever" or "whatever":

ὃς ἂν τόπος μὴ δέξηται ὑμᾶς. . . (Mark 6:11)
Whatever place does not welcome you . . .

When you see ἄν, expect a subjunctive to follow!

5. **Emphatic Negation.** The subjunctive is used following the double negative οὐ μή to express strong negation. I suggest translating οὐ μή as "in no way. . ." and the subjunctive with "may" or "will."

Did God say, "<u>In no way</u> may you eat from any tree in the garden?" (LXX Gen 3:1)
εἶπεν ὁ θεός οὐ μὴ φάγητε ἀπὸ παντὸς ξύλου τοῦ ἐν τῷ παραδείσῳς;

Even though I must die with you, <u>in no way</u> will I deny you. (Matt 26:35)
κἂν δέῃ με σὺν σοὶ ἀποθανεῖν, οὐ μή σε ἀπαρνήσομαι.

4. Recall that ἔρχομαι is *deponent in the continuous stem but not with the aorist stem!

Subjunctive—the Mood of Possibility

EXERCISES

Circle each English subjunctive in the following sentences and identify each as either *hortatory*, *deliberative*, or in a *conditional* statement. If in a conditional statement, put brackets around the *protasis.

1. Let us pray.
   προσευχώμεθα.

2. If I testify about myself, my testimony is not true. (John 5:31)
   Ἐὰν ἐγὼ μαρτυρῶ περὶ ἐμαυτοῦ, ἡ μαρτυρία μου οὐκ ἔστιν ἀληθής.

3. And even if I judge, my judgment is true. (John 8:16)
   καὶ ἐὰν κρίνω δὲ ἐγώ, ἡ κρίσις ἡ ἐμὴ ἀληθινή ἐστιν.

4. Let anyone who is thirsty come to me and drink. (John 7:37)
   ἐάν τις διψᾷ ἐρχέσθω πρός με καὶ πινέτω.

5. If you continue in my word, you are truly my disciples. (John 8:31)
   ἐὰν ὑμεῖς μείνητε ἐν τῷ λόγῳ τῷ ἐμῷ, ἀληθῶς μαθηταί μού ἐστε.

6. What should we eat? Or: What should we drink? Or: what should we wear? (Matt 6:31)
   τί φάγωμεν; ἤ· τί πίωμεν; ἤ· τί περιβαλώμεθα;

7. So if the Son makes you free, you will be free indeed. (John 8:36)
   ἐὰν οὖν ὁ υἱὸς ὑμᾶς ἐλευθερώσῃ, ὄντως ἐλεύθεροι ἔσεσθε.

8. If I glorify myself, my glory is nothing. (John 8:54)
   ἐὰν ἐγὼ δοξάσω ἐμαυτόν, ἡ δόξα μου οὐδέν ἐστιν·

9. Let us grow up in every way into him who is the head, Christ. (Eph 4:15)
   αὐξήσωμεν εἰς αὐτὸν τὰ πάντα, ὅς ἐστιν ἡ κεφαλή, Χριστός.

10. Then what if you were to see the Son of Man ascending to where he was before? (John 6:62)
ἐὰν οὖν θεωρῆτε τὸν υἱὸν τοῦ ἀνθρώπου ἀναβαίνοντα ὅπου ἦν τὸ πρότερον;

17

Infinitives—The Verbal Noun

DEVOTION

"He isn't about to journey into the diaspora of the Greeks and to teach the Greeks, is he?" (John 7:35)

μὴ εἰς τὴν διασπορὰν τῶν Ἑλλήνων μέλλει πορεύεσθαι καὶ διδάσκειν τοὺς Ἕλληνας;

The irony is rich. In the previous verses, Jesus tells the crowd that he will be with them awhile longer, but will then go to the One who sent him. He tells them "You will search for me, but you will not find me; and where I am you cannot come" (John 7:34). The crowd responds with the question quoted above, using the infinitives ("to journey" and "to teach") to complete the verb "about." They wonder if he is "about to journey and to teach," expecting the answer to be "surely not!" They misunderstand Jesus' words, thinking he's leaving Palestine to go teach the Greeks. Jesus is talking about going to the Father (compare Jesus' words to his disciples in John 14:1–7). The irony is that Jesus does teach the Greeks even in Palestine (see John 12:20–26)! Even more, the message about Jesus has journeyed out beyond the Greeks, even to you and me, bringing us life in Jesus' name.

DEFINITION: INFINITIVE

An ***Infinitive** is an indeclinable verbal noun. This means that it has aspect and voice like every verb. As an indeclinable noun it does not change its form. It can be used as a **substantive** in place of a noun, as a **complement** to complete a verbal idea, or as an **adverb** answering why, when, in what manner, etc. In English, the infinitive is formed by using the preposition "to" (e.g., "to read").

SIMILARITIES

There are three basic uses of an infinitive in both English and Greek:

1. Substantive. The infinitive is used in place of a noun.

> *To live is Christ, to die is gain. (Phil 1:21)*
> τὸ ζῆν Χριστὸς καὶ τὸ ἀποθανεῖν κέρδος.

"To live" and "to die" are both infinitives. They are the nominatives in the predicate nominative.

Sometimes substantive infinitives will be translated with "-ing," as gerunds in English. The NRSV translates Phil 1:21 that way:

> *<u>Living</u> is Christ and <u>dying</u> is gain.*

For our purposes, use "to" plus the verb to express the infinitive in Greek as an infinitive in English.

To confirm that an infinitive is substantive, try replacing it with a noun or pronoun. The meaning will change, but if the syntax is correct then it is substantive. For example:

> *<u>To live</u> is Christ => <u>He</u> is Christ*

This confirms that "to live" is functioning as a noun.

2. Complementary. In Greek and English some verbs require an infinitive to finish their thought:

> *The centurion had a slave who <u>was about to die</u>.*

The verb "was about..." requires an infinitive to finish the thought, in this case, "to die." In this case, the infinitive is complementary to the verb "was about" (in Greek μέλλω).

Other verbs that require infinitives include "I am able..." (δύναμαι) and "I am beginning..." (ἄρχομαι).

Some impersonal verbs in English also take the infinitive. ("Impersonal" means that "it" is the stated subject.) For example, "It is necessary..." (δεῖ) and "It is lawful..." (ἔξεστιν) take the infinitive.[1]

To confirm that an infinitive is complementary, try removing it. If the verb doesn't make sense anymore, then it is probably complementary. For example, remove "to die" from the above sentence:

---

1. Technically speaking, the infinitives with these verbs are substantives, which is made clear by making the infinitive the subject, e.g., "To eat is lawful for us." However, because the idea of the verb is incomplete without the infinitive, we will count them as complementary infinitives. See Croy §169, p.144 or Mounce p. 303.

INFINITIVES—THE VERBAL NOUN

The centurion had a slave who was about.

The infinitive is necessary to complete the thought; therefore, it is complementary.

3. Adverbially. Both Greek and English use the infinitive adverbially to indicate **purpose**, answering the question "why?" Greek (but not English) also uses the infinitive to indicate result and time as will be discussed below. For now, keep in mind that the infinitive can modify a verb to indicate purpose.

Jesus was going <u>to preach</u> in Judea.

The infinitive "to preach" indicates the purpose for Jesus going. To confirm this sense, substitute the preposition "to" with "in order to": Jesus was going *in order to preach* in Judea. The answer to the question, "Why was Jesus going?" is "to preach."

DIFFERENCES

1. English uses the preposition "to" before the verb to form the infinitive: "to read."

2. Greek uses one of the aspect stems (continuous, aorist, or perfect) and adds a morpheme (see Croy §170, p. 145 or Mounce p. 299). The four morphemes are:
    - -ειν (Continuous Active, 2nd Aorist Active)   λύειν
    - -σθαι (Cont. M/P, Aorist Middle, Perfect M/P) and   λύεσθαι
    - -ναι (Aorist Passive, Perfect Active)   λυθῆναι
    - -ι (1st Aorist Active)   λῦσαι

3. The **continuous aspect** in Greek may be emphasized by using "to continue to . . ." in English. For example: λύειν may be translated "to continue to loose."

4. When used as a **substantive** in Greek, the infinitive usually will be preceded by the definite article, typically the neuter singular article. For example, note the articles before the infinitives ζῆν and ἀποθανεῖν.

To live is Christ, to die is gain. (Phil 1:21)
τὸ ζῆν Χριστὸς καὶ τὸ ἀποθανεῖν κέρδος.

5. **Complementary** infinitives may be separated by some distance from the verb that it completes. Learn to look for an infinitive when you see the verbs:
    - δεῖ   it is necessary
    - ἔξεστιν   it is lawful
    - μέλλω   I am about . . .
    - δύναμαι   I am able . . .
    - ἄρχομαι   I am beginning . . .

4. The **adverbial** use of the Greek infinitive is broader than in English. We discussed above that Greek and English both use the infinitive for **purpose** (see Exercises below). Greek also uses infinitives to indicate **cause, time, and result**. These are often constructed with prepositions. Study your Greek textbook (e.g., Croy pp. 146–7 or Mounce pp. 304–5) carefully to see the various ways this works. Pay special attention to the three ways infinitives can be used to express purpose (See Croy p. 146 and Mounce p. 304). In most of these cases you will not translate the infinitive with the English preposition "to . . ." You will often use a dependent clause in English with a subject and indicative form.

5. The **"subject"** of a infinitive is in the accusative case. If you see a noun or pronoun in the accusative case near the infinitive, it may be the "subject" of the infinitive. (Recall our discussion of the "subject" of participles.) You will most often translate adverbial infinitive phrases as English dependent clauses and need this "subject." For example,

διὰ τὸ βλέπειν αὐτόν is translated *"because he sees."*

αὐτόν is in the accusative case and acts as the subject of the infinitive βλέπειν.

EXERCISES

Circle each infinitive in the following sentences and identify each as either *substantive, complementary, or purpose.*

1. To err is human, to forgive is divine.

2. The disciples were about to fall asleep.

3. You are not able to serve God and mammon.

4. Is it lawful for us to give tribute to Caesar?

5. Do not think that I came to destroy the law.

Circle each infinitive and draw brackets around the infinitive phrase, including any objects or prepositional phrases that link to the infinitive.

6. Didn't you know that it is necessary for me to be in my father's house?

Infinitives—The Verbal Noun

7. Rabbi, for us to be here is good.

8. They led him away to crucify him.

9. For me, to live is Christ and to die is gain.

10. It is easier for a camel to go through the eye of a needle . . .

18

Imperatives

DEVOTION

"Let the one who wants it take the water of life as a gift." (Rev 22:17)

ὁ θέλων λαβέτω ὕδωρ ζωῆς δωρεάν.

Economics are a central issue in the book of Revelation. Some Christians in Smyrna may be poor (Rev 2:9) while Christians in Laodicea are wealthy enough to say, "I am rich, I have prospered, and I need nothing" (Rev 3:17). These people perhaps participated in Babylon's idolatrous economy that had made kings, merchants, and sailors comfortable (Rev 18), but they also may have accepted the "mark of the beast" (e.g., worship of the Roman emperor) as a requirement to buy or sell (Rev 13:17).

In contrast, God gives the essentials of life now and forever as a gift. Jesus tells the Christians in Smyrna that they are really rich! God promises that the Lamb will lead believers to "the springs of the water of life" (Rev 7:17). They will not thirst or hunger anymore (Rev 7:16).

At the end of Revelation, John uses the 3rd person imperative "Let...take" (λαβέτω) to indicate that the one who wants this water of life should take it. It is a gift God freely offers through Jesus that sustains life now and forever.

DEFINITION: IMPERATIVE

The *Imperative mood is used to express commands, prohibitions, exhortations, and entreaties.

SIMILARITIES

1. In English and Greek, the basic function of the *imperative is to express **commands** or exhortations:

IMPERATIVES

Give to the one who asks you. (Matt 5:42)
τῷ αἰτοῦντί σε δός.

Entreaty is perhaps the better word to describe a request from someone in need who is asking for help, for example, the father with a boy possessed by an unclean spirit says to Jesus:

If you are able (to do) something, help us. (Mark 9:22)
εἴ τι δύνῃ, βοήθησον ἡμῖν.

This is the sense of the imperative mood used in **prayer**:

Give us today our daily bread. (Matt 6:11)
τὸν ἄρτον ἡμῶν τὸν ἐπιούσιον δὸς ἡμῖν σήμερον·

Negative commands are called **prohibitions**.

Do not be afraid. (Mark 6:50)
μὴ φοβεῖσθε.

2. In the above examples, the subject is **"you" (sing or plural)** although it is not explicitly stated. These are **2nd person imperatives**. The speaker is talking directly to someone. For the command, imagine Jesus pointing his finger at a disciple and saying:

(You), give to the one who asks!

Or Jesus walking across the water and saying to the frightened disciples:

(You pl.), do not be afraid.

When the imperative is used for an entreaty or prayer, imagine a person on their knees asking:

(You), give us daily bread!

3. In both English and Greek, there is a way to command indirectly, which in Greek we call the **3rd person imperative**. The subject of the 3rd person imperative is a person or thing *who is not the person spoken to,* but the person or thing that the speaker wants to act.

Imagine Jesus talking to Peter about John:

Jesus is saying to Peter, "Let John go into the house"
Ἰησοῦς λέγει τῷ Πέτρῳ, Ἰωάννης ἐρχέσθω εἰς τὸν οἶκόν.

Jesus is asking for John to go into the house, with the implication that Peter somehow is involved in John's action. The context will determine how exactly Peter is involved. For example, Peter may want to go into the house rather than John, but Jesus commands, "Let John go into the house." **The key to translating 3rd person imperatives is to use the English phrase "Let . . ."** The Lord's Prayer uses three 3rd person imperatives that may be translated:

> *Let your name <u>be made holy</u>;*
> *<u>let</u> your kingdom <u>come</u>;*
> *<u>let</u> your will <u>become</u> . . .*

> ἁγιασθήτω τὸ ὄνομά σου·
> ἐλθέτω ἡ βασιλεία σου·
> γενηθήτω τὸ θέλημά σου . . .

The person is praying to God, but the subjects of these entreaties are "your name," "your kingdom," and "your will."

DIFFERENCES

1. English imperatives are not inflected, but Greek imperatives change form.

2. Greek uses one of the Aspect Stems (Continuous, Aorist, or Perfect) and adds an imperative morpheme. The continuous aspect may be emphasized by making "continue" the imperative in English followed by the infinitive.

Cont. Act. Imper. 2nd Sing	λύ + ε = λῦε		(You) Continue to loose!
Cont. Mid. Imper. 2nd Sing	λύ + ου = λύου		(You) Continue to loose for yourself!
Cont. Pass. Imper. 2nd Sing	λύ + ου = λύου		(You) Continue to be loosed!

Note that these forms overlap with other verbal forms:
  a. the plural imperative endings are identical to the plural *indicative present* endings (-ετε, -εσθε; -τε, -σθε).
  b. the 1st aorist active imperative (λῦσαι) is identical with the 1st aorist active *infinitive* (λῦσαι).

In these cases, context will be your guide. **Context rules!** In some cases, the confusion can create some interesting exegetical observations.

3. In English, the phrase "Let . . ." often suggests permission, which is not always the force of the Greek 3rd person imperative. "The third person imperative is as strongly

IMPERATIVES

directive as the second person."[1] Sometimes the 3rd person imperative is better translated as "should" or "must," for example:

> *Are any among you sick? They <u>should call</u> for the elders of the church and <u>have them pray</u> . . . (James 5:14)*
> ἀσθενεῖ τις ἐν ὑμῖν, <u>προσκαλεσάσθω</u> τοὺς πρεσβυτέρους τῆς ἐκκλησίας καὶ <u>προσευξάσθωσαν</u> . . .

EXERCISES

Circle each imperative in the following sentences and identify each as either 2nd or 3rd person. Recall that the English translation of the 3rd person imperative often begins with "Let . . ." (circle the "let" with the verb). If it is a 3rd person imperative, <u>underline the subject</u>.

1. Father, glorify your name. (John 12:28)

2. Jesus cried out, "Let anyone who is thirsty come to me." (John 7:37)

3. Lazarus came out and Jesus said to them, "Unbind him and allow him to go." (John 11:44)

4. Do not be afraid, daughter of Zion! Look, your ruler is coming! (John 12:15)

5. If the house is worthy, let your peace come upon it, but if it is not worthy, let your peace return to you. (Matt 10:13)

6. Should I say, "Father, save me from this hour"? (John 12:27)

7. Where is the word of the Lord? Let it come! (Jer 17:15 LXX)

8. Let mutual love continue. (Heb 13:1)

---

1. See Porter, *Idioms of the Greek New Testament*, 55.

9. Walk while you have the light. (John 12:35)

10. Let the one who serves me follow me. (John 12:26)

19

Relative Pronouns—Relating a Clause to a Noun

DEVOTION

Who, although being in the form of God, did not consider being equal to God something to grasp . . . (Phil 2:6)

ὃς ἐν μορφῇ θεοῦ ὑπάρχων οὐχ ἁρπαγμὸν ἡγήσατο τὸ εἶναι ἴσα θεῷ . . .

This phrase begins a passage that provides a foundation for understanding Christ as true human and true God simultaneously. Paul emphasizes to the Philippians that Christ did not look to his own interests but became like a slave. Paul exhorts the Philippians to behave as Christ did, not out of selfish ambition but out of one mind with God, in obedience to God, and in service to others.

It is possible that Philippians 2:6–11 was sung by Christians in worship. It is often considered a hymn because it begins with a relative pronoun and uses relative pronouns to describe Jesus (also see Colossians 1:15–20). Relative pronouns are a way to describe a noun with clauses that have a subject and verb. Using relative pronouns, someone or something can be described as active and a story can be told that directly connects to that person, place, thing, or idea. In the case of Phil 2:6–11, the relative pronoun describes Jesus: it begins a long clause (a hymn!) that tells us about Jesus, who Jesus is, and what Jesus has done.

DEFINITION: RELATIVE PRONOUN

A *Relative Pronoun is a word that stands in for a noun or pronoun and begins a relative clause. Pronouns like "who," "whom," "whose," "which," "what," and "that" can be used as relative pronouns in English. Like other pronouns, the relative pronoun always refers back to a noun or pronoun, called its *antecedent. Unlike other pronouns, it begins a relative clause that modifies its antecedent. A key point is that the form of the relative pronoun reflects its function in the relative clause and not the main clause.

SIMILARITIES

1. Both Greek and English use relative pronouns **to modify nouns or pronouns with clauses**. In both Greek and English they are **the first word of the relative clause**:

> *Jesus saw the disciple whom he loved.*

The clause "whom he loved" modifies "the disciple," answering the question: "which disciple?" "Whom" is the relative pronoun that connects "whom he loved" to the clause "Jesus saw the disciple."

Like other pronouns, relative pronouns stand in for nouns. In the example above, "whom" stands in for "the disciple." Therefore, we say "the disciple" is the *antecedent of "whom."

2. In English and Greek, **the form of the relative pronoun depends on its function** in its clause. In the example above, "whom" is the object of the verb "loved." Take this example to see a different form:

> *Jesus who loved the disciple saw him.*

The relative pronoun is "who," referring to "Jesus." In its clause it is the subject of the verb "loved."

3. One of the critical steps in English and Greek is to **determine the extent of the relative clause**, what words are in the relative clause and what words are not. When you see a relative pronoun, first look for a new subject (which may be the relative pronoun in the Nominative case) and a new verb. Then look for any other words that relate to the subject or verb, such as direct objects, prepositional phrases, etc. It helps to bracket the clause:

> *Jesus [who loved the disciple] saw him.*

and to re-write the relative clause as an independent sentence, replacing the relative pronoun with its antecedent:

> *who loved the disciple => Jesus loved the disciple*

or to take the earlier example

> *whom he loved => he loved the disciple*

Note how when we replace the relative pronoun with its antecedent, it assumes the place to function properly in English.

Relative Pronouns—Relating a Clause to a Noun

After taking out the relative clause, the first clause should still make sense:[1]

Jesus saw him

If not, reconsider what words belong in the relative clause. Consider this example:

The disciple who abides in Jesus and remains in him will inherit eternal life.

The initial glance may lead one to think that the relative clause is "who abides in Jesus," but look what remains if that clause is removed:

The disciple . . . and remains in him will inherit eternal life.

The relative clause must be "who abides in Jesus and remains in him." Check by rewriting the relative clause:

The disciple abides in Jesus and remains in him.

Be sure to include all prepositions phrases, adverbs, and direct and indirect objects that are part of the predicate of the clause. Consider this example:

Jesus went to Capernaum [that was across the sea of Galilee from Gadara] and went home.

Re-write the relative clause:

Capernaum was across the sea of Galilee from Gadara.

4. In both English and Greek, it is important to see that **prepositions before relative pronouns indicate the function of the relative pronoun in its clause.** The relative clause is the object of the preposition, and so the preposition indicates the function of the relative pronoun in its clause. When you bracket a relative clause **include any preposition before the relative pronoun**. For example:

Jesus looked at Peter [about whom he had said, "You will deny me three times."]

"Whom" refers to "Peter." The preposition "about" indicates the function of the relative pronoun in the relative clause. This is made clear by re-writing it:

He had said about Peter, "you will deny me three times."

Note how the preposition must be included when the relative clause is re-written.

---

[1] Sometimes the antecedent is omitted, which means the remaining sentence would be incomplete. For example: "Your father knows what you need" (Matt 6:8).

DIFFERENCES

1. English pronouns don't generally change their form based on gender or number. **Greek relative pronouns match their antecedent in gender and number. Remember: As in English, the case indicates its function in the relative clause *not the main clause*.**

2. **Basic Greek case meanings should be applied to relative pronouns.** For example, when you see a genitive relative pronoun, start to go through the basic meanings of the genitive (kind and separation) and see if adding "of" or "from" makes sense. For dative pronouns, look at the context to see if it is a dative of interest, location, or instrument and if an English word needs to be added to make sense. Do not assume you will need to add an English word, especially following a preposition.

3. Normally, **the relative clause functions like an adjective**, modifying a noun or pronoun. When it has no antecedent, **it can function as a substantive in the main clause**—as a subject, direct object, etc. In these cases you may need to add "The one who...," "The thing that...," or some other words that help communicate its substance. For example:

> <u>The ones</u> who came spoke.
> οἵ ἦλθον εἶπον.

4. Sometimes **the case of the relative pronoun is attracted to its antecedent**, especially if the relative pronoun would naturally be accusative. For example note the genitive οὗ which matches the case of the antecedent τοῦ ὕδατος:

> *out of the water which I will give . . . (John 4:14)*
> ἐκ τοῦ ὕδατος οὗ ἐγὼ δώσω . . .

More naturally it should have had the accusative relative pronoun ὅ since it is the direct object of the verb δώσω (I will give) in the relative clause.

> ἐκ τοῦ ὕδατος ὅ ἐγὼ δώσω . . .

RECOGNITION

The easiest way to recognize the relative pronoun is to remember they generally look like the endings of the definite articles with rough breathing. Take the *tau* off and add rough breathing, and Voila! (The only exception is the nom, masc, sing ὅς.) **The key to recognition is the rough breathing.**

Relative Pronouns—Relating a Clause to a Noun

EXERCISES

Circle the relative pronoun(s). Draw brackets around the relative clause(s), including any preposition that precedes the relative pronoun. Re-write the relative clause(s) as an independent sentence, replacing the relative pronoun with its antecedent and putting it into its place for proper English word order.

1. John testified to him, "This was he of whom I spoke."

2. He on whom you see the Spirit descend and remain is the one who baptizes with the Holy Spirit."

3. We have found him about whom Moses in the law and prophets wrote.

4. Rabbi, the one who was with you across the Jordan is here.

5. Now he said this about the Spirit, which believers in him were to receive.

6. Now some of the people were saying, "Is not this the man whom they are trying to kill?"

7. All that the Father has is mine.

8. Jesus came to Bethany, the home of Lazarus, whom he had raised from the dead.

9. One of his disciples, the one whom Jesus loved, was reclining next to him.

10. Immediately the boat reached the land toward which they were going.

Appendix

For Further Study of Greek Aspect

This book promotes early awareness of the importance of aspect in understanding Greek verbal forms and translating them into English. The students who have learned this in my classes have found separating aspect and time helpful for their exegesis and conceptualization of texts. Although introductory textbooks have long noted the significance of aspect and the inaccuracy of using "tense" for non-indicative forms, they have done little to help students integrate and utilize with these fundamental concepts. Instead, the semantic and pragmatic issues have been relegated to advanced textbooks that the majority of introductory students will never see.

There is disagreement between scholars on how to best describe aspect in Greek. I speculate that this is the reason introductory textbooks hesitate to make a break from the old tense system of Greek instruction. For example, not everyone will agree with how I present the Perfect aspect in the book. Nonetheless, I suggest that introductory textbooks must start somewhere rather than allow another generation of Greek students pass through with minimal awareness of how the Greek verbal system focuses more on aspect than time, fundamentally more spatial than temporal. This appendix gives guidance for further study of this fascinating and fruitful area.

After completing an introductory Greek class, I suggest a student wishing further exposure to Greek aspect read the intermediate textbook by **Constantine R. Campbell, *Basics of Verbal Aspect in Biblical Greek***. Prof. Campbell complexifies the categories introduced in this book with the concepts of *Aktionsart*, remoteness, and proximity. He helpfully discusses the lexical dimensions of aspect for intermediate students.

For advanced students and teachers who would like to explore the debates around Greek aspect, four books would be appropriate for the next step: Stanley E. Porter, *Verbal Aspect in the Greek of the New Testament, with Reference to Tense and Mood*, Buist M. Fanning, *Verbal Aspect in New Testament Greek*, K. L. McKay, *A New Syntax of the Verb in New Testament Greek: An Aspectual Approach*, and R. J. Decker, *Temporal Deixis of the Greek Verb in the Gospel of Mark with Reference to Verbal Aspect*. These four lay out the contours of the modern debate.

For Further Study of Greek Aspect

A good summary of the discussion can be found in Porter and Carson, eds., *Biblical Greek Language and Linguistics: Open Questions in Current Research*, especially the articles by Moisés Silva, Daryl D. Schmidt, Stanley E. Porter, and Buist Fanning. Randall Buth's thoughts on helping students think in Greek and Trevor Evans guidance for future studies are found in Peter R. Burton, et. al, eds., *Biblical Greek Language and Lexicography: Essays in Honor of Fredrick W. Danker.* See the Bibliography for more references.

Answer Key to Exercises

CHAPTER 1 (GRAMMAR JARGON)

Identify the part of speech of each word in the following sentences.

1. **Jesus** **went** **beside** **the** **sea.**
   Noun   verb   preposition   article   noun

2. **The** **whole** **crowd** **gathered** **around** **him** **and**
   Article   adj.   noun   verb   prep.   pronoun   conjunction

   he **taught** **them.**
   pronoun   verb   pronoun.

3. **As** **he** **was** **walking** **along,** **he** **saw** **Levi.**
   Conj.   pron.   verb   verb   adv.   pron.   verb   noun

4. **The** **wedding** **guests** **do** **not** **fast** **while** **the** **bridegroom**
   Article   adj.   noun   verb   adv.   verb   conj.   art.   Noun

   is **with** **them,** **do** **they?**
   verb   prep.   pronoun   verb   pronoun

5. **The** **Pharisees** **said** **to** **him,** **"Look!** **Why** **are** **they**
   Art.   noun.   verb   prep.   pron.   interjection   adv.   verb   pron.

   doing **what** **is** **not** **lawful** **on** **the** **Sabbath?"**
   verb   pron.   verb   adv.   adj.   prep.   art.   Noun

113

Answer Key to Exercises

Identify the subject and predicate of the following sentences. Be sure to indicate the whole subject—it may be more than one word.

*The **subject** is shown in bold face. All other words in the sentence are the predicate.*

6. **Jesus** departed with his disciples to the sea.

7. **John the baptizer** appeared in the wilderness.

8. **A great multitude from Galilee** followed him.

9. **People from the whole Judean countryside and all the people of Jerusalem** were going out to him.

10. That evening, at sundown, **they** brought to him all who were sick or possessed with demons.

CHAPTER 2 (VERBS)

Circle the finite verb(s) in English, meaning verbs that have person and number. Be sure you circle the whole *verb phrase, which may be more than one word. Next to each finite verb **write its time (past, present, future), person (1st, 2nd, 3rd) and number (singular, plural).**

1. When he entered the temple, the chief priests came to him.
   entered = past, 3rd, singular (matching "he")
   came = past, 3rd, plural (matching "priests")

2. They said, "By what authority are you doing these things?"
   said = past, 3rd, plural (matching "they")
   are doing = present, 2nd, singular (matching "you")

Answer Key to Exercises

3. Jesus said to them, "I will also ask you one question."
   said = past, 3rd, singular (matching "Jesus")
   will ask = future, 1st, singular (matching "I")

4. If you tell me the answer, then I will also tell you.
   tell = present, 2nd, plural (in context, matching "priests")
   will tell = future, 1st, singular (matching "I")

5. Did the baptism of John come from heaven?
   did come = past, 3rd, singular (matching "baptism")

6. And they argued with one another.
   argued = past, 3rd, plural (matching "they")

7. They said, "If we say, 'From heaven,' he will say to us, . . ."
   said = past, 3rd, plural (matching "they")
   say = present, 1st, plural (matching "we")
   will say = future, 3rd, singular (matching "he")

8. "Why did you not believe him?"
   did believe = past, 2nd, plural (in context, matching "they")
   Note that "not" is an adverb modifying this verb phrase and technically not a part of it.

9. We are afraid of the crowd, because they all regard John as a prophet.
   are afraid = present, 1st, plural (matching "we")
   regard = present, 3rd, plural (matching "they")

10. So they answered Jesus, "We do not know."
    answered = past, 3rd, plural (matching "they")
    do know = present, 1st, plural (matching "we")

ANSWER KEY TO EXERCISES

CHAPTER 3 (CONTINUOUS ACTIVE INDICATIVE PRESENT)

Rewrite the following sentences in English to emphasize continuous action of the verb. In general, you will need to use some form of "be" with a participle.

1. Jesus returns to Capernaum.
   Jesus is returning to Capernaum.

2. Many people gather around the home.
   Many people are gathering around the home.

3. He speaks the word to them.
   He is speaking the word to them.

4. Four people bring a paralyzed man to him.
   Four people are bringing a paralyzed man to him.

5. They dig through the roof above him.
   They are digging through the roof above him.

6. They let down the mat.
   They are letting down the mat.

7. Jesus forgives the man's sins.
   Jesus is forgiving the man's sins.

8. Some scribes question in their hearts.
   Some scribes are questioning in their hearts.

9. Jesus perceives their thoughts.
   Jesus is perceiving their thoughts.

10. The man stands up and takes the mat.
    The man is standing up and is taking the mat.

CHAPTER 4 (NOMINATIVE AND ACCUSATIVE)

Look at the underlined English word and use the names of Greek cases (only nominative or accusative for these examples) to *parse the underlined word, giving the case, number, gender, and *lexical form (in English). The idea is to begin to think in Greek categories. For these examples we'll follow English gender, so list the gender as neuter unless it is "naturally" masculine or feminine. **Write ? when it is not possible to determine the number or gender without more context.**

1. <u>John</u> was standing with two of his disciples.

   Case: <u>Nom.</u> Number: <u>Sing.</u>   Gender: <u>Masc.</u>   Lexical Form: <u>John</u>

2. The two disciples heard <u>him</u>.

   Case: <u>Acc.</u> Number: <u>Sing.</u>   Gender: <u>Masc.</u>   Lexical Form: <u>he</u>

3. The <u>speech</u> of Christ stirred my heart.

   Case: <u>Nom.</u> Number: <u>Sing.</u>   Gender: <u>Neut (Eng)</u>   Lexical Form: <u>speech</u>

4. A Samaritan <u>woman</u> came to draw water.

   Case: <u>Nom.</u> Number: <u>Sing.</u>   Gender: <u>Fem.</u>   Lexical Form: <u>woman</u>

5. <u>The disciples</u> were urging Jesus to eat something.

   Case: <u>Nom.</u> Number: <u>Plural</u> Gender: <u>?</u>   Lexical Form: <u>disciple</u>

6. For by grace <u>you</u> have been saved through faith.
   Τῇ γὰρ χάριτί ἐστε σεσῳσμένοι διὰ πίστεως· (Eph 2:8)

   Case: <u>Nom.</u> Number: <u>? (Pl in Gk)</u>   Gender: <u>?</u>   Lexical Form: <u>you</u>

Answer Key to Exercises

7. And they sent to him their <u>disciples</u> . . .
   καὶ ἀποστέλλουσιν αὐτῷ τοὺς <u>μαθητὰς</u> αὐτῶν . . . (Matt 22:16)

   Case: <u>Acc.</u>   Number: <u>Plural</u>   Gender: ? <u>(Masc in Gk)</u>   Lexical Form: <u>disciple</u>

8. And getting <u>a sponge</u>, filling it with sour wine . . .
   λαβὼν <u>σπόγγον</u> πλήσας τε ὄξους . . . (Matt 27:48)

   Case: <u>Acc.</u>   Number: <u>Sing.</u>   Gender: ? <u>(Neut in Gk)</u>   Lexical Form: <u>sponge</u>

9. <u>They</u> went into the house of Simon and Andrew.
   ἦλθον εἰς τὴν οἰκίαν Σίμωνος καὶ Ἀνδρέου. (Mark 1:29)

   Case: <u>Nom</u>   Number: <u>Plural</u>   Gender: ?   Lexical Form: <u>he/she</u>

10. Are <u>you</u> greater than our father Jacob?
    μὴ σὺ μείζων εἶ τοῦ πατρὸς ἡμῶν Ἰακώβ; (John 4:2)

    Case: <u>Nom</u>   Number: <u>? (Sing in Gk)</u>   Gender: ?   Lexical Form: <u>you</u>

CHAPTER 5 (GENITIVE AND DATIVE)

Identify how the underlined words function in the sentence using the categories described above (e.g., genitive of possession or dative of association).

1. The woman gave the Greek book <u>to the man</u>.
   Dative of interest: indirect object

2. The book <u>of vocabulary</u> was heavier than he thought.
   Genitive of kind: content

3. The <u>speech of Christ</u> stirred my heart.
   Ambiguous: Genitive of source (Speech from Christ) or objective genitive (speech about Christ) or subjective genitive (speech that Christ spoke). Need more context to decide.

Answer Key to Exercises

4. Jesus went to Jerusalem <u>with his disciples</u>.
   Dative of Association

5. For <u>by grace</u> you have been saved through faith.
   <u>Τῇ</u> γὰρ <u>χάριτί</u> ἐστε σεσῳσμένοι διὰ πίστεως· (Eph 2:8)
   Dative of Means

6. He cried <u>in a loud voice</u> . . .
   <u>φωνῇ μεγάλῃ</u> ἐκραύγασεν . . . (John 11:43)
   Dative of Manner

7. And they sent <u>to him</u> <u>their</u> disciples . . .
   καὶ ἀποστέλλουσιν <u>αὐτῷ</u> τοὺς μαθητὰς <u>αὐτῶν</u> . . . (Matt 22:16)
   Dative of interest: indirect object; genitive of kind: relationship

8. And getting a sponge, filling it <u>with sour wine</u> . . .
   λαβὼν σπόγγον πλήσας τε <u>ὄξους</u> . . . (Matt 27:48 Note genitive translated "with")
   Genitive of kind: Content

9. They went into the house <u>of Simon and Andrew</u> . . .
   ἦλθον εἰς τὴν οἰκίαν <u>Σίμωνος καὶ Ἀνδρέου</u> . . . (Mark 1:29)
   Genitive of kind: Possession

10. Are you greater <u>than our father Jacob</u>?
    μὴ σὺ μείζων εἶ <u>τοῦ πατρὸς ἡμῶν Ἰακώβ</u>; (John 4:2; The indeclinable noun Ἰακώβ is also genitive. There are two more.)
    Genitive of Comparison ("than"); genitive of kind: possession

CHAPTER 6 (ADJECTIVES)

Circle the adjective(s) (underlined here). Write above whether the adjective is attributive, predicate, or substantive. If attributive or predicate, draw an arrow from the adjective to the noun it modifies in the following sentences.

Answer Key to Exercises

1. A large crowd kept following him.
   large = attributive modifying "crowd"

2. The well is deep.
   deep = predicate modifying "well"

3. There is a boy who has five loaves and two fish.
   five = attributive modifying "loaves"; two = attributive modifying fish

4. He cried with a loud voice, "Lazarus, come out!"
   loud = attributive modifying "voice"

5. Now a man was ill.
   ill = predicate modifying "man"

6. The true light was coming into the world. (John 2:12)
   Ἦν τὸ φῶς τὸ ἀληθινόν ἐρχόμενον εἰς τὸν κόσμον.
   true = attributive modifying "light"

7. I am not worthy to untie the thong of his sandal. (John 1:27)
   οὐκ εἰμί ἐγὼ ἄξιος ἵνα λύσω αὐτοῦ τὸν ἱμάντα τοῦ ὑποδήματος.
   worthy = predicate modifying "I"

8. I will raise them up on the last day . . . (John 6:39)
   ἀναστήσω αὐτοὺς ἐν τῇ ἐσχάτῃ ἡμέρᾳ . . .
   last = attributive modifying "day"

9. And another sign was seen in heaven: behold! A great red dragon! (Rev 12:3)
   καὶ ὤφθη ἄλλο σημεῖον ἐν τῷ οὐρανῷ, καὶ ἰδοὺ δράκων μέγας πυρρός.
   another = attributive modifying "sign"
   great = attributive modifying "dragon"
   red = attributive modifying "dragon"

10. Five of them were foolish and five were wise... (Matt 25:2)
    πέντε δὲ ἐξ αὐτῶν ἦσαν μωραὶ καὶ πέντε φρόνιμοι...
    Five = substantive, for five people (women in this case)
    foolish = predicate modifying the first "five"
    wise = predicate modifying the second "five"

CHAPTER 7 (PREPOSITIONS)

Circle the preposition(s) and underline the prepositional phrase(s) in the following sentences. Prepositions are boldfaced, the phrase underlined in the answer key.

1. I fell asleep **on** my book.

2. I took my Greek flash cards **with** me.

3. The student is climbing **up** a steep hill.

4. The jogger ran **around** the block and fell down **on** the ground **in** exhaustion.

5. The coat that his father had put **over** his head was torn and thrown **out of** reach.

6. There was a wedding **in** Cana of Galilee. (John 2:1a)[1]
   γάμος ἐγένετο **ἐν** Κανὰ τῆς Γαλιλαίας.

7. And the Word was **with** God. (John 1:1b)
   καὶ ὁ λόγος ἦν **πρὸς** τὸν θεόν.

8. After this he went down **to** Capernaum. (John 2:12)
   Μετὰ τοῦτο κατέβη **εἰς** Καφαρναοὺμ αὐτός.

---

[1]. Technically, 'of' is a preposition in English. We won't be marking it, however, because there is not an equivalent preposition in Greek. If you circle 'of' it is correct, but keep in mind the difference with Greek.

9. And he spent some time there **with** them. (John 3:22)
   καὶ ἐκεῖ διέτριβεν **μετ' αὐτῶν**.

10. **Before** Philip called you,[2] I saw you **under** the fig tree. (Jn 1:48)
    πρὸ τοῦ σε Φίλιππον φωνῆσαι ὄντα **ὑπὸ τὴν συκῆν** εἶδόν σε.

CHAPTER 8 (PRONOUNS)

Circle the pronoun(s) in John 2 (the Wedding of Cana). Write its person (1st, 2nd or 3rd) next to the circle. If the noun that it is replacing is in context (including other sentences), draw an arrow to it from the pronoun.

1. Jesus and his disciples had been invited to the wedding.
   his = 3rd person masc. sing. referring to Jesus

2. And the mother of Jesus said to him, "They have no wine."
   him = 3rd person masc. sing. referring to Jesus
   they = 3rd person plural referring to ? (no clear antecedent: could be attendees, hosts, servants?)

3. And Jesus said to her, "Woman, what concern is that to you and to me?"
   her = 3rd person fem. sing. referring to mother
   you = 2nd person sing. referring to mother
   me = 1st person sing. referring to Jesus

4. "My hour has not yet come."
   my = 1st person sing. referring to Jesus

5. His mother said to the servants:
   his = 3rd person masc. sing. referring to Jesus

---

2. Here, the preposition introduces a dependent clause "Before Philip called you." We'll see more of this later.

6. "Do whatever he tells you."
   he = 3rd person masc. sing. referring to Jesus
   you = 2nd person plural. referring to servants

7. Jesus said to them, "Fill the jars with water."
   them = 3rd person plural. referring to servants

8. And they filled them up to the brim.
   they = 3rd person plural referring to servants
   them = 3rd person plural referring to jars

9. When the steward tasted the water, he did not know where it came from.
   he = 3rd person masc. sing. referring to the steward
   it = 3rd person neut. sing. referring to water

10. The steward called the bridegroom and said to him, "Everyone serves good wine first."
    him = 3rd person masc. sing. referring to Jesus

CHAPTER 9 (PASSIVE VOICE)

Rewrite the following sentences, changing verbs from *active voice* to *passive voice*. Be sure to keep the time of the verb the same.

1. God will wipe away every tear.
   Every tear will be wiped away by God.

2. Jesus healed the man.
   The man was healed by Jesus.

3. The disciples threw the net on the other side of the boat.
   The net was thrown by the disciples on the other side of the boat.

Answer Key to Exercises

4. Lydia provided a place for Paul to rest.
   A place was provided by Lydia for Paul to rest.

5. After taking bread, he broke it.
   After bread was taken, it was broken by him.

Rewrite the following sentences, changing verbs from the *passive voice* to *active voice*. For some examples, you will have to infer God or another as the agent. Be sure that you keep the time of the verb the same.

6. He was baptized in the river by John.
   John baptized him in the river.

7. The man's sins were forgiven by Jesus.
   Jesus forgave the man's sins.

8. Paul was sent by the Holy Spirit to Macedonia.
   The Holy Spirit sent Paul to Macedonia.

9. They were given white robes.
   (God) gave them white robes. (Divine Passive?)

10. They will be called children of God.
    (God) will call them children of God. (Divine Passive?)

CHAPTER 10 (MIDDLE VOICE)

Practice translating the following Greek deponent verbs as active. Some verbs have prepositional prefixes; separate the prefix first to see the verbal stem and then translate. These are all continuous present—so make sure you emphasize the continuous aspect!

1. ἔρχεται
   he/she/it is coming/going

2. δύνανται
   they are able

3. γίνεται
   he/she/it is becoming

4. διερχόμεθα = διά + ἔρχ-ομαι
   we are going/coming through

5. εἰσέρχονται = εἰς + ἔρχ-ομαι
   they are going/coming into

6. ἀποκρίνεσθε
   you (pl.) are answering

7. πορεύομαι
   I am traveling

8. ἄρχεσθε
   you (pl.) are beginning

9. ἐκπορεύομαι = ἐκ + πορεύ-ομαι
   I am traveling out of

10. βούλεται
    he/she/it is wishing

Rewrite the following sentences into an equivalent of the middle voice by removing the direct object or indirect object and replacing it with a form of *self* that reflects back on the subject.

11. She washed her children.
    She washes herself.

12. They taught the disciples the word of the Lord.
    They taught themselves the word of the Lord.

13. Mary chose the best for Martha (i.e., "for Martha's benefit").
    Mary chose the best for herself.

14. You received the truth for them (i.e., "for their benefit")
    You received the truth for yourself.

15. They will be called children of God.
    They will call themselves children of God.

CHAPTER 11 (CONTINUOUS PAST)

Rewrite the following sentences, changing verbs in the *continuous present* to the *continuous past*.

1. Jesus is coming to Bethany.
   Jesus was coming to Bethany.

2. There they are giving him a dinner.
   There they were giving him a dinner.

3. Martha is serving and Lazarus is sitting at the table.
   Martha was serving and Lazarus was sitting at the table.

4. Mary is taking a pound of costly perfume and is anointing his feet.
   Mary was taking a pound of costly perfume and was anointing his feet.

5. Jesus' feet are wiped by her hair. *(What case would "hair" be in Greek?)*
   Jesus' feet were being wiped by her hair. ("hair" is the instrument used for wiping, so most likely the dative case)

Answer Key to Exercises

Rewrite the following sentences, changing verbs from the *simple (aorist) past* to the *continuous past*. If you think the action could be customary, try including "used to" in the translation. If you think the action could be persistent, try including "kept on."

6. The house filled with the fragrance of the perfume.
   The house was filling with the fragrance of the perfume.

7. But Judas Iscariot complained.
   But Judas Iscariot was complaining.
   Or, to emphasize persistent action in the past: *But Judas Iscariot kept on complaining.*

8. He said this not because he cared about the poor, but because he stole from the common purse.
   He was saying this not because he was caring about the poor, but because he was stealing from the common purse.
   Or, to emphasize customary action in the past: *He was saying this not because he used to care about the poor, but because he used to steal from the common purse.*

9. Jesus said, "She bought it for the day of my burial."
   Jesus said, "She was buying it for the day of my burial."

10. So the chief priests planned to put Lazarus to death as well.
    So the chief priests were planning to put Lazarus to death as well.

CHAPTER 12 (FUTURE TIME)

Rewrite the following sentences, changing verbs in *past time into future time*.

1. Jesus looked at the rich man, and loved him.
   Jesus will look at the rich man, and will love him.

2. Teacher, I have kept all the commandments.
   Teacher, I will keep all the commandments.

3. You lacked one thing.
   You will lack one thing.

4. When he heard this, he was shocked.
   When he will hear this, he will be shocked.

5. And he went away grieving because he had many possessions.
   And he will go away grieving because he will have many possessions.

Rewrite the following sentences, changing verbs from the *future time to present time*. Emphasize a continuous aspect when you write the verb in present time.

6. You shall not murder.
   You are not murdering.

7. You will give him the name Jesus, because he will save his people from their sins.
   You are giving him the name Jesus, because he is saving his people from their sins.

8. Not one stone will be left on another, for all will be thrown down.
   Not one stone is being left on another, for all are being thrown down.

9. How hard it will be for those who have wealth to enter the kingdom of God!
   How hard it is for those who have wealth to enter the kingdom of God!

10. Then, who will be saved?
    Then, who is being saved?

CHAPTER 13 (AORIST ASPECT)

Rewrite the following sentences, changing verbs in the *continuous past* to the *aorist past*.

Answer Key to Exercises

1. Jesus was coming to Galilee.
   Jesus came to Galilee.

2. He was testifying the word of God.
   He testified the word of God.

3. The Galileans were welcoming him.
   The Galileans welcomed him.

4. They were seeing everything he was doing at the festival.
   They saw everything he did at the festival.

5. They also were going to the festival.
   They also went to the festival.

Rewrite the following sentences, changing verbs from the *aorist past* to the *continuous past*. If you think the action could be customary, try including "used to" in the translation. If you think the action could be persistent, try including "kept on."

6. Then he came to Cana in Galilee.
   Then he was coming to Cana in Galilee.

7. A royal official heard that Jesus came to Galilee.
   A royal official was hearing that Jesus was coming to Galilee.

8. He begged him to heal his son.
   He was begging him to heal his son or *He kept on begging him to heal his son.*

9. Jesus said to him, "Will you believe if you see signs?"
   Jesus was saying to him, "Will you believe if you see signs?"

10. The man believed the word that Jesus spoke to him.
    The man was believing the word that Jesus was speaking to him.

Answer Key to Exercises

CHAPTER 14 (PERFECT ASPECT)

Rewrite the following sentences, changing verbs in the *aorist past* to the *perfect present*.

1. I wrote about all that Jesus did and taught.
   I have written about all that Jesus has done and has taught.

2. Jesus was taken up into heaven.
   Jesus has been taken up to heaven. (note voice)

3. He gave instructions through the Holy Spirit to the apostles whom he chose.
   He has given instructions through the Holy Spirit to the apostles whom he has chosen.

4. After he suffered, he presented himself alive to them.
   After he has suffered, he has presented himself alive to them.
   (The perfect past "he had suffered" with the aorist "he presented" makes more sense in English, but the exercise is using the perfect present).

5. He appeared to them for forty days and spoke about the royal rule of God.
   He has appeared to them for forty days and has spoken about the royal rule of God.

Rewrite the following sentences, changing verbs from the *perfect present* to the *aorist past*.

6. While he has stayed with them, he has ordered them not to leave Jerusalem.
   While he stayed with them, he ordered them not to leave Jerusalem.

7. Instead, they have waited there for the promise of the Father.
   Instead, they waited there for the promise of the Father.

Answer Key to Exercises

8. He has said, "This is what you have heard from me.
   He said, "This is what you heard from me.

9. John has baptized with water, but you will be baptized with the Holy Spirit.
   John baptized with water, but you will be baptized with the Holy Spirit."

10. When they have come together, they have asked him many questions.
    When they came together, they asked him many questions.

CHAPTER 15 (PARTICIPLES)

Circle each participle in the following sentences and identify each as either *substantive, periphrastic, attributive* or *adverbial*.

1. God will judge the living and the dead.
   living = substantive

2. The running father threw his arms around his son.
   running = attributive, modifying noun "father"

3. His son begged for forgiveness, weeping and wailing.
   weeping, wailing = adverbial, modifying verb "begged"

4. The woman is drawing water from the deep well.
   drawing = periphrastic (note follows form of "be")

5. Jesus offers her living water.
   living = attributive, modifying "water"

Circle each participle and draw brackets around the participial phrase, including any objects or prepositional phrases that link to the participle. *Participles are underlined below.*

6. Every eye will see the one [coming on the clouds].
   Substantive

7. The tax collector confessed his sin, [hanging his head in shame].
   Adverbial, modifying "confessed"

8. The one [believing in him] will have eternal life.
   Substantive

9. [Kneeling before Jesus], the rich man asked, "What must I do?"
   Adverbial, modifying "asked"

10. Jesus said, "Everyone [hearing my word] and [doing it] is like a wise man [building his house on rock.]"
    "Hearing" and "doing" are attributive to "everyone"
    "building" is attributive, modifying "person"

CHAPTER 16 (SUBJUNCTIVE)

Circle (underlined below) each English subjunctive in the following sentences and identify each as either *hortatory, deliberative* or in a *conditional* statement. If in a conditional statement, put brackets around the *protasis.

1. Let us pray.
   Hortatory

2. [If I testify about myself], my testimony is not true. (John 5:31)
   Conditional

3. And [even if I judge], my judgment is true. (John 8:16)
   Conditional

4. Let anyone who is <u>thirsty</u> come to me and drink. (John 7:37)
   Hortatory

5. [If you <u>continue</u> in my word], you are truly my disciples. (John 8:31)
   Conditional

6. What should we <u>eat</u>? Or: What should we <u>drink</u>? Or: what should we <u>wear</u>? (Matt 6:31)
   Deliberative

7. So [if the Son <u>makes</u> you free], you will be free indeed. (John 8:36)
   Conditional

8. [If I <u>glorify</u> myself], my glory is nothing. (John 8:54)
   Conditional

9. Let us <u>grow</u> up in every way into him who is the head, Christ. (Eph 4:15)
   Hortatory

10. Then what [if you <u>were</u> to see the Son of Man ascending to where he was before]? (John 6:62)
    Conditional. Note that the apodosis is omitted, but implied in context!

CHAPTER 17 (INFINITIVES)

Circle each infinitive in the following sentences and identify each as either *substantive, complementary, or purpose*. Infinitives are underlined below.

1. <u>To err</u> is human, <u>to forgive</u> is divine.
   Both are substantives.

2. The disciples were about <u>to fall asleep</u>.
   Complementary to "were about." The verbal idea is incomplete without the infinitive.

Answer Key to Exercises

3. You are not able <u>to serve</u> God and mammon.
   Complementary to "are able."

4. Is it lawful for us <u>to give</u> tribute to Caesar?
   Complementary to "is lawful."[3]

5. Do not think that I came <u>to destroy</u> the law.
   Purpose. Note that "I came" makes sense without the infinitive, which supplies the purpose of coming.

Circle each infinitive and draw brackets around the infinitive phrase, including any objects or prepositional phrases that link to the infinitive.

6. Didn't you know that it is necessary for me [<u>to be</u> in my father's house]?
   Complementary to "is necessary."[4]

7. Rabbi, for us [<u>to be</u> here] is good.
   Substantive.

8. They led him away [<u>to crucify</u> him].
   Purpose.

9. For me, [<u>to live</u>] is Christ and [<u>to die</u>] is gain.
   Both are substantives.

10. It is easier for a camel [<u>to go</u> through the eye of a needle] . . .
    Substantive. Note that "easier" is a comparative adjective, and so this is a predicate nominative and can be rewritten "To go through the eye of a needle is easier for a camel. . ."

---

[3] Technically "to give" is substantive and the subject of the impersonal verb "is lawful", which is seen if one rewrites the sentence "To give tribute to Caesar is lawful for us." In Greek this is also true for the verbs ἔξεστιν (it is lawful), δεί (it is necessary), δοκεί (it seems), etc. See Wallace, *Greek Grammar: Beyond the Basics*, 600. For our purposes, we will follow Mounce, 304, who calls the use of the infinitive complementary with these verbs.

[4] See note 3 above.

ANSWER KEY TO EXERCISES

CHAPTER 18 (IMPERATIVES)

Circle each imperative in the following sentences and identify each as either *2nd or 3rd person*. Recall that the English translation of the 3rd person imperative often begins with "Let. . ." (circle the "let" with the verb). If it is a 3rd person imperative, <u>underline the subject</u>.

1. Father, glorify your name. (John 12:28)
   Glorify = 2nd person

2. Jesus cried out, "Let <u>anyone who is thirsty</u> come to me." (John 7:37)
   Let come = 3rd person

3. Lazarus came out and Jesus said to them, "Unbind him and allow him to go." (John 11:44)
   Unbind, allow = 2nd person

4. Do not be afraid, daughter of Zion! Look, your ruler is coming! (John 12:15)
   Do not be afraid = 2nd person (I suggest including "not" to recognize that this is a prohibition)
   Look = 2nd person

5. If the house is worthy, let <u>your peace</u> come upon it, but if it is not worthy, let <u>your peace</u> return to you. (Matt 10:13)
   let come, let return = 3rd person

6. Should I say, "Father, save me from this hour"? (John 12:27)
   save = 2nd person

7. Where is the word of the Lord? Let <u>it</u> come! (Jer 17:15 LXX)
   Let come = 3rd person

8. Let <u>mutual love</u> continue. (Heb 13:1)
   Let continue = 3rd person

9. Walk while you have the light. (John 12:35)
   Walk = 2nd person

10. Let the one who serves me follow me. (John 12:26)
    Let follow = 3rd person

CHAPTER 19 (RELATIVE PRONOUNS)

Circle the relative pronoun(s). Draw brackets around the relative clause(s), including any preposition that precedes the relative pronoun. Re-write the relative clause(s) as an independent sentence, replacing the relative pronoun with its antecedent and putting it into its place for proper English word order.

1. John testified to him, "This was he [of whom I spoke]."
   I spoke of him.

2. He [on whom you see the Spirit descend and remain] is the one [who baptizes with the Holy Spirit]."
   You see the Spirit descend and remain on him.
   He baptizes with the Holy Spirit.

3. We have found him [about whom Moses in the law and prophets wrote].
   Moses in the law and prophets wrote about him.

4. Rabbi, the one [who was with you across the Jordan] is here.
   He/she (not clear with only this sentence) was with you across the Jordan.

5. Now he said this about the Spirit, [which believers in him were to receive].
   Believers in him were to receive the Spirit.

6. Now some of the people were saying, "Is not this the man [whom they are trying to kill]?"
   They are trying to kill the man.

Answer Key to Exercises

7. All [that the Father has] is mine.
   The Father has all.

8. Jesus came to Bethany, the home of Lazarus, [whom he had raised from the dead].
   He has raised Lazarus from the dead.

9. One of his disciples, the one [whom Jesus loved], was reclining next to him.
   Jesus loved him/her (one of the disciples).

10. Immediately the boat reached the land [toward which they were going].
    They were going toward the land.

Glossary

The ***Active voice** communicates that the *subject is the same as the *agent. The *agent is the one who does the action.

An ***Adjective** is a word used with a noun to describe it, indicate it, or count the number. Another way to detect an adjective is to put the word *very* in front of it (there are some exceptions). Adjectives often answer the questions: *What kind? How many? How much? Which? Whose? In what order?*

An ***Adverb** is a word that modifies all parts of speech except *nouns. Adverbs often answer *When? Where? How?* or intensify a word. In English, many adverbs end in "-ly."

The ***Agent** is the doer of the action in a *passive voice construction.

The ***Antecedent** is the *noun or noun substitute to which a *pronoun refers. Sometimes the antecedent may be difficult to determine—and this becomes exegetically exciting!

The ***apodosis** is the clause expressing the consequence of a conditional statement (think ἀπό = "away from" the condition).

The ***Aorist Aspect** indicates "simple," or "undefined" action. In Greek, the word "aorist" means "undefined." This aspect is undefined in the sense that its viewpoint must be determined in context. In general, we can say that the aorist aspect views the action from the outside, and can focus on various parts of the action or the action as a whole. It can view the beginning of the action, its end, or the whole action. The aorist may refer to:

the beginning of an action (represented by an arrow at the beginning of the line):

↑
_____

the end of an action (represented by an arrow at the end of a line):

_____
↑

Glossary

or the whole action (represented solely by a dot):

•
↑

***Articles** are joined to nouns like adjectives. They are easier to list than define: the definite article is "the" and in English we use "a" or "an" as indefinite articles. (There is no indefinite article in Greek.)

***Aspect** refers to the verb's point of view of the action, especially in respect to continuity and completion. Every verbal form (finite and non-finite) has aspect in Greek.

A ***Conjunction** is a word that joins *sentences, *clauses, *phrases, or words. When you see a conjunction ask what it connects. "And," "but," and "or" are the three most common, but "because," "although," "thus," "therefore," "as," "while," etc. are also conjunctions in English. The main idea is that they link words, phrases, and clauses.

The ***Continuous Aspect** (some people call it progressive or incomplete) describes a point of view inside the action, with no sense of its completion, beginning or end. In English the continuous aspect is expressed using an auxiliary verb (usually some form of "be," such as "am," "are," "was," etc.) and a participle (a verbal form with "-ing"). This aspect can be represented by a straight line:

―――――――――――

The continuous aspect also can suggest habitual or repeated action without sense of beginning or end. In this case, English does not express the continuous aspect except by the implication of habit or repetition.

In this case, the continuous aspect can be represented by a series of dashes:

- -

***Declension** is a summary of the way the form of a word changes when customarily used.

***Deponent** verbs are *middle voice in form, but *active in meaning. *Deponent is not technically a voice, but I encourage you to note "deponent" when parsing these verbs.

A ***Finite verb** is a word used to make a statement about a *noun, ask a question, or make a command. It is called "finite" because it refers to a specific noun (the subject) and must agree with that *subject in *person and *number.

Glossary

*__Future time__ refers to action that, at the time of speaking, has not yet taken place. In English, we generally add "will" to the verb to indicate future time.

*__Grammar__ is the study of the basic principles of a language, which include *Morphology and *Syntax, and the meaning resulting from forming and arranging words.

*__Historic Present__ refers to a present time verb used to refer to events in the past at the time of telling. In storytelling, the present time is sometimes to help the audience feel like the story is taking place at that very minute, even if it refers to past events.

The *__Imperative mood__ is used for commands and instructions.

The *__Imperfect Tense__ is what we are calling "continuous past."

The *__Indicative mood__ is used for ordinary statements and questions. It "indicates" something, referring to actual facts in time. The Indicative mood is generally the only mood with *time (discussed further below).

*__Infinitives__ are verbal nouns. In English, we add "to" before a word to make an infinitive. Infinitives are non-finite, meaning they do not have a person or number.

*__Inflected__ refers to a word that changes form based on its function; from a Latin root which means "bent."

An *__Interjection__ is a word thrown into a sentence to express a feeling. It has no grammatical relationship with any other word. For example, ἰδού (behold)!

The *__Lexical Form__ is the form of the word that you will find in a lexicon or dictionary.

The *__Middle Voice__ indicates that the grammatical subject of the verb is *both* the *agent (the doer of the action) and in some way the *receiver of the action (what is acted upon). For example "I shaved" implies "I shaved *myself*."

The *__Mood__ of a verb expresses the speaker/author's perception of the reality of the action of the verb. The indicative, imperative, subjunctive, and optative are all finite forms (they have person and number). Although infinitives and participles aren't technically moods, it is traditional to include these non-finite forms under the category of mood.

*__Morphology__ is the way individual words are formed.

A *__Noun__ is a name for anything. Another way to detect a noun is to see if it can fill in this blank: "The _____ is good". Some nouns are concrete, such as *boat, rock, net*. Others are abstract: *love, joy, peace*. Some nouns are derived from adjectives or verbs: "*Decision*" is derived from the verb "decide." "*Happiness*" is derived from the adjective "happy."

Glossary

The ***Number** of a noun, pronoun, or verb indicates whether it is singular or plural.

The ***Optative mood** is rare in the NT. It is used to express a wish or hope. The most common in the NT is μὴ γένοιτο, usually translated "By no means!" (e.g., Rom 6:1).

*__Participial Phrases__. Because participles are verb forms, they can have direct objects and indirect objects and be modified by adverbs and prepositional phrases. When you see a participle, look for these things and bracket the participial phrase in order to avoid confusion.

*__Participles__ are verbal adjectives. In English, we generally add "-ing" to the verb to make a participle.

*__Parts of Speech__ are some ways to classify words based on their common function. We discuss nine: *noun, *pronoun, *adjective, *verb, *adverb, *preposition, *conjunction, *interjection, *article.

*__Parsing__ is describing the form of a word. For each part of speech there is a scheme for parsing, like blanks to be filled. For *articles, *nouns, and *adjectives there are four blanks to fill:

Case: ____ Number: ____ Gender: ____ Lexical Form: ____

For *verbs there are up to seven blanks to fill (not all blanks will be filled in for each form. (See chapter 8, especially the parsing chart.) Every verb will include at least the following:

Aspect: ____ Voice: ____ Mood: ____ Lexical Form: ____

The *__Passive voice__ communicates that the *subject of the verb is the direct object of the action. In English, we use some form of "be" with a past participle. In Greek the passive voice is indicated in the form of the verb. In English and Greek, the agent may be omitted or communicated using the preposition "by" (ὑπό in Greek). The use of the passive voice may be exegetically significant because it generally emphasizes the object of the verb over the agent of the action.

*__Past time__ refers to an action that happened prior to the time when the speaker spoke the sentence.

The *__Perfect Aspect__ (or "completed") emphasizes an action that has reached its natural conclusion and has some enduring effect or result. In English, we add forms of the auxiliary "have" to a participle to make the perfect aspect. In general, it is helpful to

Glossary

think of the perfect like a dot (the action) followed by a line of enduring effects up until a certain point:

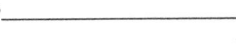

*Periphrastic. "Peri" (around) + "phrasis" (speaking) simply means "a round about way of speaking," or using more words than necessary to say something. In this case, some form of "be" may be used with a participle to communicate the same thing as a single verb. In English, we use periphrasis for the continuous aspect: Jesus *is coming*.

The **Person* of a verb or pronoun indicates the relationship with the speaker or audience. There are three classes of persons:
  1st person "I" or "we" (the speaker refers to her- or himself);
  2nd person "you" (the speaker refers to audience, singular, or plural);
  3rd person "she," "he," "it" (singular) or "they" (plural) (the speaker refers to someone or something other than self or audience).

The **Pluperfect* is what we are calling "Perfect Past."

The **Predicate* is everything that follows the *subject, beginning with the *verb.

A **Preposition* is a word that indicates the relationship between two *nouns (or equivalents). It is followed by a word or phrase we call **the object of the preposition**. Together this phrase is called a **Prepositional Phrase*, and functions as either an *adjective or *adverb. Another test of a preposition is that it can be placed before "her" and "them" but not "she" and "they."

*Present time refers to action contemporary with speaking.

A **Pronoun* is a word that stands in for a noun. The noun that is replaced is called the *antecedent. Some pronouns include *I, you, they, who, that, this*.

The **protasis* is the "if" clause in a conditional statement, the clause expressing the condition (think πρό = "in front of").

The **Receiver* of the action is what is acted upon in a *passive or *middle voice construction.

*Reflexive pronouns reflect back on the subject, for example *myself, himself, herself,* and *themselves.*

The **Subject* is what the *Verb agrees with in number, or another way to say it: the subject is what determines whether the verb is singular or plural. One way to find the verb

Glossary

is to put **what** or **who** in front of the Verb and turn it into a question. The answer to the question is the subject. The **whole subject** may be more than one word.

The ***Subjunctive mood** expresses potential rather than actual facts. In general, we use auxiliaries like "may" or "might" with the verb for the subjunctive in English. This is somewhat an unreliable way to translate the Greek subjunctive, but don't worry about that now. The subjunctive is especially important in some conditional statements ("if . . . then").

***Substantive** refers to when an *adjective, *participle, or *infinitive is used in place of a noun, sometimes with an article.

***Syntax** is the way that multiple words are arranged to form sentences.

***Time** applies only to verbs in the *indicative mood that indicate facts or ask questions. There are three times: *past, *present, and *future.

A ***Verb** is a word used to make a statement about a *noun, ask a question, or make a command. It must agree with the *subject in *person and *number.

A ***Verb Phrase** includes helping words (sometimes called auxiliaries or modals) such as *shall, can, may, might, should, would, must* and *ought to*. Some verbs (such as *is, have, do* and *get*) may function as auxiliaries.

***Voice** refers to the relationship between the grammatical *subject of the verb and the *agent of the action.

Bibliography

Bluedorn, Harvey. *A Review of English Grammar for Students of Biblical Greek (and other Ancient Languages)*. New Boston, IL: Trivium, 2008.
Brown, Raymond. *The Gospel According to John I-XII*. AB 29. New York: Doubleday, 1966.
Croy, Clayton. *A Primer of Biblical Greek*. Grand Rapids: Eerdmans, 1999.
Lamerson, Samuel. *English Grammar to Ace New Testament Greek*. Grand Rapids: Zondervan, 2004.
Mounce, William D. *Basics of Biblical Greek*. 3rd ed. Grand Rapids: Zondervan, 2009.
Nunn, H. P. V. *A Short Syntax of New Testament Greek*. Cambridge: Cambridge University Press, 1951.
Porter, Stanley E. *Idioms of the Greek New Testament*. New York: Continuum, 1992.
Smyth, Herbert Weir. *Greek Grammar*. Cambridge, MA: Harvard University Press, 1956.
Williams, Joseph M. *Style: Ten Lessons in Clarity and Grace*. New York: Longman, 2000.

FURTHER READING ON GREEK ASPECT

Burton, Peter R., et al., eds. *Biblical Greek Language and Lexicography: Essays in Honor of Fredrick W. Danker*. Grand Rapids: Eerdmans, 2004.
Buth, Randall. "Verbs Perception and Aspect, Greek Lexicography and Grammar: Helping Students think in Greek." In *Biblical Greek Language and Lexicography: Essays in Honor of Fredrick W. Danker*, edited by Peter R. Burton et al., 177–98. Grand Rapids: Eerdmans, 2004.
Campbell, Constantine R. *Basics of Verbal Aspect in Biblical Greek*. Grand Rapids: Zondervan, 2008.
Comrie, Bernard. *Aspect: An Introduction to the Study of Verbal Aspect and Related Problems*. Cambridge: Cambridge University Press, 1976.
Decker, R. J. *Temporal Deixis of the Greek Verb in the Gospel of Mark with Reference to Verbal Aspect*. New York: Peter Lang, 2001.
Evans, Trevor V. "Future Directions for Aspect Studies in Ancient Greek." In *Biblical Greek Language and Lexicography: Essays in Honor of Fredrick W. Danker*, edited by Peter R. Burton et al., 199–206. Grand Rapids: Eerdmans, 2004.
———. *Verbal Syntax in the Greek Pentateuch: Natural Greek Usage and Hebrew Interference*. Oxford: Oxford University Press, 2001.
Fanning, Buist M. *Verbal Aspect in New Testament Greek*. Oxford: Clarendon, 1990.
McKay, K. L. *A New Syntax of the Verb in New Testament Greek: An Aspectual Approach*. New York: Peter Lang, 1994.
Porter, Stanley E. *Verbal Aspect in the Greek of the New Testament, with Reference to Tense and Mood*. 2nd ed. Studies in Biblical Greek 1. New York: Peter Lang, 1993.
Porter, Stanley E. and D. A. Carson, eds. *Biblical Greek Language and Linguistics: Open Questions in Current Research*. JSNTSup 80. Sheffield: Sheffield Academic, 1993.
Sicking, C. M. J. and Peter Stork. *Two Studies in the Semantics of the Verb in Classical Greek*. Leiden: Brill, 1996.
Stork, Peter. *The Aspectual Usage of the Dynamic Infinitive in Herodotus*. Groningen: Bouma, 1982.
Verkuyl, H. J. *A Theory of Aspectuality: The Interaction between Temporal and Atemporal Sequence*. Cambridge: Cambridge University Press, 1993.

www.ingramcontent.com/pod-product-compliance
Lightning Source LLC
Chambersburg PA
CBHW081133170426
43197CB00017B/2841